Base-Ball

How To Become A Player

John Montgomery Ward

BASE-BALL

HOW TO BECOME A PLAYER

WITH THE

ORIGIN, HISTORY, AND EXPLANATION OF THE
GAME

BY

JOHN MONTGOMERY WARD

OF THE

NEW YORK BASE-BALL CLUB.

ILLUSTRATED.

PHILADELPHIA
THE ATHLETIC PUBLISHING COMPANY
No. 1124 ARCH STREET
1888

FOREWORD

When John Montgomery Ward wrote *Base-Ball: Ho·v to Become a Player*, he was one of the game's best known practitioners himself. In 1888, the year of publication, his New York Giants would win the National League pennant and the World Series against the St. Louis Browns of the American Association. Ward, by this time a shortstop, had been a force to be reckoned with since coming up as a pitcher with Providence at the age of 18 in 1878. He went 22-13 in his rookie season, then boosted the Grays to the World Championship with a 47-19 record the next year. In 1880, he pitched the majors' second perfect game five days after John Lee Richmond of Worcester pitched the first. His effectiveness in the box waned, and he began to play more often in the outfield.

Ward (who was usually called "Johnnie" in his playing days, not "Monte" as most references have it) moved to New York in 1883, and the next season a baserunning injury to his right arm ended his pitching career for good. He played the outfield briefly lefthanded. When his right arm strengthened, he shifted to the infield, and captained New York in the mid-1880s.

Ward wasn't your run-of-the mill baseball star. On one hand, in an era of rugged individualists, his personality was even pricklier than most (George Wright, his manager at Providence, called him "obstinate"). He exhibited a hot temper and a ferocious desire to win. He punched an umpire, fought with opposing players, and was heartily disliked by teammates like Buck Ewing and Tim Keefe.

On the other hand, Ward was a sophisticated man about town, a Columbia-trained lawyer considered by many proper "downtown" fans to be a rare gentleman among a mob of drunken louts. He had, in 1887, married the famous and beautiful actress Helen Dauvray, and that same year had penned the basic document in the long war between players and owners. "Is the Base-Ball Player a Chattel?", which appeared in *Lippencott's Magazine* put the issue of the Reserve Rule plainly before the public—and maybe more important, plainly before the players themselves.

The article was written after Al Spalding of Chicago sold Mike "King" Kelly to Boston for the staggering sum of $10,000, and used the reserve rule to claim the right to keep all the money.

This event, and Ward's angry, well-reasoned article boosted membership in the Brotherhood of Professional Baseball Players, the organization Ward and a few teammates had founded two years earlier. The Brotherhood didn't originally oppose the reserve system, and it's clear in *Base-Ball: How to Become a Player* that Ward himself had mixed feelings on the subject as late as 1888. But while Ward was traveling with Spalding's World Tour over the off-season of 1888-89, the owners instituted the Brush Classification Plan, the purpose of which was to restrict players' salaries. A showdown was inevitable.

In the fall of 1889, Ward announced the formation of the Players' National League of Professional Base Ball Clubs, which is usually known as the Players' League. Whole rosters jumped from the National League, and almost every great player in the game threw in his lot with the Brotherhood. Ultimately one man, Al Spalding, saved the National League's bacon with his business acumen and his personal fortune. The Players' League, which had seemed to have won the war during the season of 1890, lost the peace that fall and winter.

Ward remained in the game as a player and manager through 1894, and then put his legal training to use full time, swiftly becoming a prominent member of the New York Bar. He and his second wife bought a Long Island estate and he became an early exponent of a sport that would claim the hearts of many future players—golf. Ward continued to speak out on baseball matters, and he represented many players who had disputes with their clubs. In fact, a majority of National League owners were ready to elect him league president in 1909, but powerful American League president Ban Johnson used his clout to block him because Ward had represented his former teammate George Davis in a contract dispute with the Chicago White Sox.

In later years, Ward was briefly president of the Boston Braves, and in the mid-teens, he went to baseball war again as business manager of the Brooklyn franchise in the Federal League. He died in 1925, and was voted into the Baseball Hall of Fame in 1964.

Base-Ball: How to Become a Player is one of the best books about baseball ever written by a player. Ward was a thinker, an innovator, a close observer—and, rarest of all, a decent writer. He loved the game, was a major actor in some of its most dramatic events, and played on the field during its transition into its modern form. His brief history of the game, which leads this book, was probably the best available at the time—a sensible and valuable look at the development of baseball flawed only by Ward's chauvinistic insistence that our game was a purely American sport, not descended from or related to English ball and bat games.

The book is a wonderful window on an era that we all too often regard as quaint—when we don't ignore it altogether. In many ways, the game wasn't that different a hundred and five years ago. You'll find Ward describing the brushback (I bet there wasn't anything quaint about getting dusted off by a fastball from what amounted to 55-1/2 feet). He discusses the hit-and-run (without naming it), playing the infield in, pitching signs, and the pickoff. He affirms that bases are stolen off the pitcher, not the catcher, and he treats the question of whether a curve ball curves as a settled matter.

Of course, much has changed. You'll be intrigued by Ward's discussions of the batting and fielding techniques of particular players. You'll be reminded how different the game was before fielders wore gloves and the catcher was fully protected. And you'll enjoy a feeling for baseball when there were "yet many unsettled points."

Enough of this. All you need to do is turn a few pages to be hooked on your own.

Mark Alvarez
Publications Director
SABR

PREFACE.

The author ventures to present this book to the public, because he believes there are many points in the game of base-ball which can be told only by a player. He has given some space to a consideration of the origin and early history of the game, because they are subjects deserving of more attention than is generally accorded them.

His principal aim, however, has been to produce a hand-book of the game, a picture of the play as seen by a player. In many of its branches, base-ball is still in its infancy; even in the actual play there are yet many unsettled points, and the opinions of experts differ upon important questions. The author has been as accurate as the nature of the subject would permit, and, though claiming no especial consideration for his own opinions, he thinks they will coincide in substance with those of the more experienced and intelligent players.

To Messrs. A. H. Wright, Henry Chadwick, Harry Wright, and James Whyte Davis, for materials of reference, and to Goodwin & Co., the *Scientific American*, and A. J. Reach, for engravings and cuts, acknowledgments are gratefully made.

JOHN M. WARD.

CONTENTS.

___

INTRODUCTION.

CHAPTER I.

CHAPTER II.

CHAPTER III.

CHAPTER IV.

CHAPTER V.

CHAPTER VI.

INTRODUCTION.

AN INQUIRY INTO THE ORIGIN OF BASE-BALL, WITH A
BRIEF SKETCH OF ITS HISTORY.

It may or it may not be a serious reflection upon
the accuracy of history that the circumstances
of the invention of the first ball are enveloped
in some doubt. Herodotus attributes it to the
Lydians, but several other writers unite in con-
ceding to a certain beautiful lady of Corcyra,
Anagalla by name, the credit of first having
made a ball for the purpose of pastime. Several passages in Homer rather sustain this latter
view, and, therefore, with the weight of evidence,
and to the glory of woman, we, too, shall adopt this
theory. Anagalla did not apply for letters patent,
but, whether from goodness of heart or inability to
keep a secret, she lost no time in making known her
invention and explaining its uses. Homer, then,
relates how

> " O'er the green mead the sporting virgins play,
> Their shining veils unbound; along the skies,
> Tost and retost, the ball incessant flies."

And this is the first ball game on record, though
it is perhaps unnecessary to say that it was not yet
base-ball.

9

No other single accident has ever been so produc-
tive of games as that invention. From the day
when the Phæacian maidens started the ball rolling
down to the present time, it has been continuously
in motion, and as long as children love play and
adults feel the need of exercise and recreation, it
will continue to roll. It has been known in all
lands, and at one time or another been popular with
all peoples. The Greeks and the Romans were
great devotees of ball-play ; China was noted for her
players ; in the courts of Italy and France, we are
told, it was in especial favor, and Fitz-Stephen, writing in the 13th century, speaks of the London school-
boys playing at " the celebrated game of ball."

For many centuries no bat was known, but in those
games requiring the ball to be struck, the hand alone
was used. In France there was early played a
species of hand-ball. To protect the hands thongs
were sometimes bound about them, and this eventually furnished the idea of the racquet. Strutt thinks
a bat was first used in golf, cambuc, or bandy ball.
This was similar to the boys' game of " shinny," or,
as it is now more elegantly known, " polo," and the
bat used was bent at the end, just as now. The first
straight bats were used in the old English game
called club ball. This was simply " fungo hitting,"
in which one player tossed the ball in the air and hit
it, as it fell, to others who caught it, or sometimes it
was pitched to him by another player.

Concerning the origin of the American game of
base-ball there exists considerable uncertainty. A
correspondent of Porter's *Spirit of the Times*, as far
back as 1856, begins a series of letters on the game

by acknowledging his utter inability to arrive at any satisfactory conclusion upon this point ; and a writer of recent date introduces a research into the history of the game with the frank avowal that he has only succeeded in finding "a remarkable lack of literature on the subject."

In view of its extraordinary growth and popularity as "Our National Game," the author deems it important that its true origin should, if possible, be ascertained, and he has, therefore, devoted to this inquiry more space than might at first seem necessary.

In 1856, within a dozen years from the time of the systematization of the game, the number of clubs in the metropolitan district and the enthusiasm attending their matches began to attract particular attention. The fact became apparent that it was surely superseding the English game of cricket, and the adherents of the lattter game looked with ill-concealed jealousy on the rising upstart. There were then, as now, persons who believed that everything good and beautiful in the world must be of English origin, and these at once felt the need of a pedigree for the new game. Some one of them discovered that in certain features it resembled an English game called "rounders," and immediately it was announced to the American public that base-ball was only the English game transposed. This theory was not admitted by the followers of the new game, but, unfortunately, they were not in a position to emphasize the denial. One of the strongest advocates of the rounder theory, an Englishman-born himself, was the writer for out-door sports on the principal metropolitan publications. In this capacity and as

the author of a number of independent works of his
own, and the writer of the " base-ball " articles in several encyclopedias and books of sport, he has lost no
opportunity to advance his pet theory. Subsequent
writers have, blindly, it would seem, followed this
lead, until now we find it asserted on every hand as
a fact established by some indisputable evidence ;
and yet there has never been adduced a particle of
proof to support this conclusion.

While the author of this work entertains the greatest respect for that gentleman, both as a journalist
and man, and believes that base-ball owes to him a
monument of gratitude for the brave fight he has
always made against the enemies and abuses of the
game, he yet considers this point as to the game's
origin worthy of further investigation, and he still
regards it as an open question.

When was base-ball first played in America ?

The first contribution which in any way refers to
the antiquity of the game is the first official report
of the " National Association " in 1858.   This declares " The game of base-ball has *long* been a favorite and popular recreation in this country, but it is
only within the last fifteen years that any attempt
has been made to systematize and regulate the
game."   The italics are inserted to call attention to
the fact that in the memory of the men of that day
base-ball had been played a long time prior to 1845,
so long that the fifteen years of systematized play
was referred to by an " only."

Colonel Jas. Lee, elected an honorary member of the
Knickerbocker Club in 1846, said that he had often
played the same game when a boy, and at that time

he was a man of sixty or more years. Mr. Wm. F. Ladd, my informant, one of the original members of the Knickerbockers, says that he never in any way doubted Colonel Lee's declaration, because he was a gentleman eminently worthy of belief.

Dr. Oliver Wendell Holmes, several years since, said to the reporter of a Boston paper that base-ball was one of the sports of his college days at Harvard, and Dr. Holmes graduated in 1829.

Mr. Charles De Bost, the catcher and captain of the old Knickerbockers, played base-ball on Long Island fifty years ago, and it was the same game which the Knickerbockers afterward played.

In the absence of any recorded proof as to the antiquity of the game, testimony such as the foregoing becomes important, and it might be multiplied to an unlimited extent.

Another noticeable point is the belief in the minds of the game's first organizers that they were dealing with a purely American production, and the firmness of this conviction is evidenced by everything they said and did. An examination of the speeches and proceedings of the conventions, of articles in the daily and other periodical publications, of the poetry which the game at that early day inspired, taken in connection with the declarations of members of the first clubs still living, will show this vein of belief running all the way through. The idea that base-ball owed its origin to any foreign game was not only not entertained, but indignantly repudiated by the men of that time ; and in pursuing his investigations the writer has discovered that this feeling still exists in a most emphatic form.

In view of the foregoing we may safely say that base-ball was played in America as early, at least, as the beginning of this century.

It may be instructive now to inquire as to the antiquity of the " *old* English game" from which base-ball is said to have sprung. Deferring for the present the consideration of its resemblance to base-ball, what proof have we of its venerable existence? Looking, primarily, to the *first* editions of *old* English authorities on out-door sports, I have been unable to find any record that such a game as "rounders" was known. I may have been unfortunate in my searches, for, though I have exhausted every available source of information, I have not discovered any mention of it.

The first standard English writer to speak of rounders is "Stonehenge" in his *Manual of Sports*, London, 1856. Since then almost every English work on out-door sports describes the " old [with an emphasis] English game of rounders," and in the same connection declares it to be the germ of the American base-ball; and yet, curiously enough, not one of them gives us any authority even for dubbing it " old," much less for calling it the origin of our game. But in 1856 base-ball had been played here for many years; it had already attracted attention as the popular sport, and by 1860 was known in slightly differing forms all over the country. To all these later English writers, therefore, its existence and general principles must have been familiar, and it is consequently remarkable that, in view of their claim, they have given us no more particulars of the game of rounders. Are we to accept this assertion without reserve, when an investigation would seem to indicate that base-ball is really the older game? If this English game was then a common school-boy sport, as now claimed, it seems almost incredible that it should have escaped the notice of all the writers of the first half of the century ; and yet no sooner does base-ball become famous as the American game than English writers discover that there is an old and popular English game from which it is descended. Many of the games which the earlier writers describe are ex-tremely simple as compared with rounders, and yet the latter game is entirely overlooked!

But upon what ground have these later writers based their assumption? Many, doubtless, have simply followed the writings from this side of the Atlantic ; others have been misled by their ignorance of the actual age of our game, for there are even many Americans who think base-ball was *introduced* by the Knickerbocker and following clubs ; a few, with the proverbial insular idea, have concluded that base-ball must be of English origin, if for no other reason, because it ought to be.

It is not my intention to declare the *old* game of rounders a myth. There is ample living testimony to its existence as early perhaps as 1830, but that it was a popular English game before base-ball was played here I am not yet ready to believe. Before we accept the statement that base-ball is "only a species of glorified rounders," we should demand some proof that the latter is really the older game. In this connection it will be important to remember that there were two English games called "round-ers," but entirely distinct the one from the other.

Johnson's *Dictionary*, edition of 1876, describes the first, and presumably the older, as similar to "fives" or hand-ball, while the second is the game supposed to be allied to base-ball. "Fives" is one of the oldest of games, and if it or a similar game was called "rounders," it will require something more than the mere occurrence of the name in some old writing to prove that the game referred to is the "rounders" as now played. And if this cannot be shown, why might we not claim, with as much reason as the other theory has been maintained, that the "old English game of rounders" is only a poor imitation of the older American game of base-ball?

Up to this point we have waived the question of resemblance between the two games, but let us now inquire what are the points of similarity.

Are these, after all, so striking as to warrant the assumption that one game was derived from the other, no matter which may be shown to be the older? In each there are "sides;" the ball is tossed to the striker, who hits it with a bat; he is out if the ball so hit is caught; he runs to different bases in succession and may be put out if hit by the ball when between the bases. But with this the resemblance ceases. In base-ball nine men constitute a side, while in rounders there may be any number over three. In base-ball there are four bases (including the home), and the field is a diamond. In rounders the bases are five in number and the field a pentagon in shape. There is a fair and foul hit in base-ball, while in rounders no such thing is known. In rounders if a ball is struck at and missed, or if hit so that it falls back of the striker, he is out, while in base-ball the ball must be missed *three* times and the third one *caught* in order to retire the striker ; and a foul, unless caught like any other ball, has no effect and is simply declared "dead." In rounders the score is reckoned by counting one for each base made, and some of the authorities say the run is completed when the runner has reached the base next on the left of the one started from. In base-ball one point is scored only when the runner has made every base in succession and returned to the one from which he started. In rounders every player on the side must be put out before the other side can come in, while in base-ball from time immemorial the rule has been " three out, all out." The distinctive feature of rounders, and the one which gives it its name, is that when all of a side except two have been retired, one of the two remaining may call for "the rounder ;" that is, he is allowed three hits at the ball, and if in any one of these he can make the entire round of the bases, all the players of his side are reinstated as batters. No such feature as this was ever heard of in base-ball, yet, as said, it is the characteristic which gives to rounders its name, and any derivation of that game must certainly have preserved it.

If the points of resemblance were confined solely to these two games it would prove nothing except that boys' ideas as well as men's often run in the same channels. The very ancient game of bandy ball has its double in an older Persian sport, and the records of literary and mechanical invention present some curious coincidences. But, as a matter of fact, every point common to these two, games was known and

2

used long before in other popular sports. That the ball was tossed to the bat to be hit was true of a number of other games, among which were club ball, tip cat, and cricket ; in both of the latter and also in stool ball bases were run, and in tip cat, a game of much greater antiquity than either base-ball or rounders, the runner was out if hit by the ball when between bases. In all of these games the striker was out if the ball when hit was caught. Indeed, a comparison will show that there are as many features of base-ball common to cricket or tip cat as there are to rounders.

In view, then, of these facts, that the points of similarity are not distinctive, and that the points of difference are decidedly so, I can see no reason in analogy to say that one game is descended from the other, no matter which may be shown to be the older.

There was a game known in some parts of this country fifty or more years ago called town-ball. In 1831 a club was regularly organized in Philadelphia to play the game, and it is recorded that the first day for practice enough members were not present to make up town-ball, and so a game of "two-old-cat" was played. This town-ball was so nearly like rounders that one must have been the prototype of the other, but town-ball and base-ball were two very different games. When this same town-ball club decided in 1860 to adopt base-ball instead, many of its principal members resigned, so great was the enmity to the latter game. Never, until recently, was the assertion made that base-ball was a development of town-ball, and it could not have been done had the writers looked up at all the historical facts.

The latest attempt to fasten an English tab on the American game is noteworthy. Not content to stand by the theory that our game is sprung from the English rounders, it is now intimated that base-ball itself, the same game and under the same name, is of English origin. To complete the chain, it is now only necessary for some English writer to tell us that " in 1845 a number of English gentlemen sojourning in New York organized a club called the Knickbockers, and introduced to Americans the old English game of base-ball." This new departure has not yet gained much headway, but it must be noticed on account of the circumstances of its appearance.

The edition of *Chambers' Encyclopedia* just out, in its article on "base-ball" says that the game was mentioned in Miss Austen's *Northanger Abbey*, written about 1798, and leaves us to infer that it was the same game that we now know by that name. It was not necessary to go into the realm of fiction to find this ancient use of the name. A writer to the London *Times* in 1874 pointed out that in 1748 the *family* of Frederick, Prince of Wales, were represented as engaged in a game of base-ball. Miss Austen refers to base-ball as played by the *daughters* of " Mrs. Morland," the eldest of whom was fourteen. In Blaine's *Rural Sports*, London, 1852, in an introduction to ball games in general, occurs this passage : " There are few of us *of either sex* but have engaged in base-ball since our majority." Whether in all these cases the same game was meant matters not, and it is not established by the mere identity of names. " Base," as meaning a place of safety, dates its origin from the game of "prisoners' base" long before anything in the shape of base-ball or rounders ; so that any game of ball in which bases were a feature would likely be known by that name. The fact that in the three instances in which we find the name mentioned it is always a game for girls or women, would justify the suspicion that it was not always the same game, and that it in any way resembled our game is not to be imagined. Base-ball in its mildest form is essentially a robust game, and it would require an elastic imagination to conceive of little girls possessed of physical powers such as its play demands.

Besides, if the English base-ball of 1748, 1798, and 1852 were the same as our base-ball we would have been informed of that fact long ago, and it would never have been necessary to attribute the origin of our game to rounders. And when, in 1874, the American players were introducing base-ball to Englishmen, the patriotic Britain would not have said, as he then did, that our game was "only rounders with the rounder left out," but he would at once have told us that base-ball itself was an old English game.

But this latest theory is altogether untenable and only entitled to consideration on account of the authority under which it is put forth.

In a little book called *Jolly Games for Happy Homes*, London, 1875, dedicated to "wee little babies and grown-up ladies," there is described a game called "base-ball." It is very similar in its essence to our game and is probably a reflection of it. It is played by a number of girls in a garden or field. Having chosen sides, the "leader" of the

" out " side tosses the ball to one of the " ins," who strikes it with her hand and then scampers for the trees, posts, or other objects previously designated as bases. Having recovered the ball, the "scouts," or those on the " outs," give chase and try to hit the fleeing one at a time when she is between bases. There must be some other means, not stated, for putting out the side ; the ability to throw a ball with accuracy is vouchsafed to few girls, and if the change of innings depended upon this, the game, like a Chinese play, would probably never end. It is described, however, as a charming pastime, and, notwithstanding its simplicity, is doubtless a modern English conception of our National Game.

To recapitulate briefly, the assertion that base-ball is descended from rounders is a pure assumption, unsupported even by proof that the latter game antedates the former and unjustified by any line of reasoning based upon the likeness of the games. The other attempt to declare base-ball itself an out-and-out English game is scarcely worthy of serious consideration.

But if base-ball is neither sprung from rounders nor taken bodily from another English game, what is its origin ? I believe it to be a fruit of the inventive genius of the American boy. Like our system of government, it is an American evolution, and while, like that, it has doubtless been affected by foreign associations, it is none the less distinctively our own. Place in the hands of youth a ball and bat, and they will invent games of ball, and that these will be affected by other familiar games and in many respects resemble them, goes without saying.

The tradition among the earliest players of the game now living, is that the root from which came our present base-ball was the old-time American game of "cat-ball." This was the original American ball game, and the time when it was not played here is beyond the memory of living man. There were two varieties of the game, the first called "one-old-cat," or one-cornered-cat, and the other "two-old-cat."

In one-old-cat there were a batter, pitcher, catcher, and fielders. There were no "sides," and generally no bases to run, but in every other respect the game was like base-ball. The batter was out if he missed three times and the third strike was caught, or if the ball when hit was caught on the fly or first bound. When the striker was "put out" the catcher went in to bat, the pitcher to catch, and the first fielder to pitch, and so on again when the next striker was retired. The order of succession had been established when the players went on the field by each calling out a number, as "one," "two," "three," etc., *one* being the batter, *two* the catcher, *three* the pitcher, *four* the first fielder, etc. Thus, each in order secured his turn "at bat," the coveted position. Sometimes, when the party was larger, more than one striker was allowed, and in that case, not only to give the idle striker something to do, but to offer extra chances for putting him out, one or more bases were laid out, and having hit the ball he was forced to run to these. If he could be hit with the ball at any time when he was between bases he was out, and he was forced to be back to the striker's position in time to take his turn at bat. This made him take chances in running. No count was kept of runs. Two-old-cat differed from one-old-cat in having two batters at opposite stations, as in the old English stool-ball and the more modern cricket, while the fielders divided so that half faced one batter and half the other.

From one-old-cat to base-ball is a short step. It was only necessary to choose sides, and then the count of runs made by each would form the natural test of superiority. That base-ball actually did develop in this way was the generally accepted theory for many years.

In 1869 an article in *The Nation*, from A. H. Sedgwick, commenting upon the features of base-ball and cricket as exemplifying national characteristics, said: "To those other objectors who would contend that our explanation supposes a gradual modification of the English into the American game, while it is a matter of common learning that the latter is of no foreign origin but the lineal descendant of that favorite of boyhood, ' two-old-cat,' we would say that, fully agreeing with them as to the historical fact, we have always believed it to be so clear as not to need further evidence, and that for the purposes of this article the history of the matter is out of place."

Without going further into a consideration that might be greatly prolonged, I reassert my belief that our national game is a home production. In the field of out-door sports the American boy is easily capable of devising his own amusements, and until some proof is adduced that base-ball is not his invention I protest against this systematic effort to rob him of his dues.

The recorded history of the game may be briefly sketched ; it is not the object here to give a succinct history :

In 1845 a number of gentlemen who had been in the habit, for several years, of playing base-ball for recreation, determined to form themselves into a permanent organization under the name of "The Knickerbocker Club." They drew up a Constitution and By-laws, and scattered through the latter are to be found the first written rules of the game. They little thought that that beginning would develop into the present vast system of organized base-ball. They were guilty of no crafty changes of any foreign game; there was no incentive for that. They recorded the rules of the game as they remembered them from boyhood and as they found them in vogue at that time. For six years the club played regularly at the Elysian Field, the two nines being made up from all the members present. From 1851 other clubs began to be organized, and we find the Washington, Gotham (into which the Washington was merged), Eagle, Empire, Putnam, Baltic, Union, Mutual, Excelsior, Atlantic, Eckford, and many other clubs following in the space of a few years.

In Philadelphia town-ball was the favorite pastime and kept out base-ball for some time, while in Boston the local "New England game," as played by the Olympic, Elm Tree, and Green Mountain Clubs, deferred the introduction of base-ball, or, as it was called, "the New York game," until 1857.

Base-ball grew rapidly in favor ; the field was ripe. America needed a live out-door sport, and this game exactly suited the national temperament. It required all the manly qualities of activity, endurance, pluck, and skill peculiar to cricket, and was immeasurably superior to that game in exciting features. There were dash, spirit, and variety, and it required only a couple of hours to play a game. Developed by American brains, it was fitted to us, and we took to it with all the enthusiasm peculiar to our nature.

In 1857 a convention of delegates from sixteen clubs located in and around New York and Brooklyn was held, and a uniform set of rules drawn up to govern the play of all the clubs.

In 1858 a second general convention was held, at which twenty-five clubs were represented. A committee was appointed to formulate a Constitution and By-laws for a permanent organization, and in accordance with this "The National Association of Base-ball Players" was duly organized. The game now made rapid strides. It was no boys' sport, for no one under twenty-one years of age could be a delegate. Each year a committee of men having a practical knowledge of the game revised the playing rules, so that these were always kept abreast of the time.

During 1858 a series of three games between picked nines from New York and Brooklyn was played on the Fashion Course, Long Island. The public interest in these games was very great and the local feeling ran high. The series, which terminated in favor of New York, two to one, attracted general attention to the game.

In 1861 a similar game was played called "the silver ball match," on account of the trophy, a silver ball, offered by the New York *Clipper*. This time

Brooklyn won easily, and it is said some 15,000 people were present.

At the second annual meeting of the "National Association" in 1860, seventy clubs had delegates present, representing New York, Brooklyn, Boston, Detroit, New Haven, Newark, Troy, Albany, Buffalo, and other cities. During this year the first extended trip was taken by the Excelsior Club, of Brooklyn, going to Albany, Troy, Buffalo, Rochester, and Newburgh. All the expenses of the trip were paid from the treasury of the traveling club, for there were no inclosed grounds in those days and no questions as to percentage or guarantee were yet agitating the clubs and public. The Excelsiors won every game, and their skillful display and gentlemanly appearance did much to popularize the game in the cities visited.

Already in 1860 the game was coming to be recognized as our national pastime, and there were clubs in all the principal cities. Philadelphia had forsaken her town-ball, and Boston's "New England" game, after a hard fight, gave way to the "New York" game. Washington, Baltimore, Troy, Albany, Syracuse, Rochester, Buffalo, all had their champion teams. From Detroit to New Orleans, and from Portland, Maine, to far-off San Francisco, the grand game was the reigning out-door sport.

With the outbreak of the Civil War came a very general suspension of play in the different cities, though the records of occasional games in camp show that "the boys" did not entirely forget the old love. In 1865 the friendly contests were resumed, though the call of the rolls showed many "absent" who had never been known to miss a game. More than one of those who went out in '61 had proven his courage on the crimson field.

During the seasons of '65, '66, and '67 amateur base-ball, so-called, was in the height of its glory. At the annual Convention of the National Association in '66 a total of two hundred and two clubs from seventeen States and the District of Columbia were represented ; besides, there were present delegates from the Northwestern and Pennsylvania Associations, representing in addition over two hundred clubs.

In 1867 the trip of the "Nationals" of Washington was the first visit of an Eastern club to the West, and helped greatly to spread the reputation of the game.

For a number of years, however, certain baneful influences had crept into the game and now began to work out their legitimate effect.

The greatest of these evils was in the amount of gambling on the results of games. With so much money at stake, the public knew that players would be tampered with, and when finally its suspicions were confirmed, it refused further to patronize the game.

The construction of inclosed grounds and the charge of admission proved another danger. No regular salaries were paid, so that the players who were depending on a share of the "gate" arranged to win and lose a game in order that the deciding contest might draw well.

Doubtless there were more of these things existing in the public imagination than in actual fact, but distrust once aroused, there was no faith left for anything or anybody.

Very early in the history of the Association the practice prevailed among certain clubs of offering inducements to crack players in order to secure them as members. The clubs which could afford this grew disproportionately strong, and in the face of continual defeat the weaker clubs were losing interest. In 1859 a rule was made forbidding the participation in any matches of paid players, but it was so easily evaded that it was a dead letter. In 1866 the rule was reworded, but with no improved effect, and in 1868 the National Association decided, as the only way out of the dilemma, to recognize the professional class of players. By making this distinction it would no longer be considered a disgrace for an amateur to be beaten by a professional nine.

For the professionals the change was most beneficial. It legitimized their occupation and left them at liberty to pursue openly and honorably what they had before been forced to follow under false colors. The proud record of the Cincinnati "Reds" in '69 proved that professional base-ball could be honestly and profitably conducted, and from that time forth it was an established institution.

But with the introduction of professionalism there began a great competition for players, and this brought in a new evil in the form of "revolvers," or, as they were sometimes called, "shooting stars." Players under contract with one club yielded to the temptations of larger offers and repudiated the first agreements. It became evident that a closer organization was necessary to deal with these affairs.

In 1871 the professional and amateur organizations concluded to dissolve partnership. Two distinct associations were formed, and the first regular championship contests were engaged in by the Professional Association. After a few years the Amateur National Association passed out of existence.

In 1876 eight clubs of the " Professional National Association" formed an independent body, calling themselves " The National League," and this is the present senior base-ball organization.

In 1881 a new body of professional clubs, The American Association, entered the field, and is now, with the National League, one of the controlling factors of the game.

There have been a number of other base-ball associations formed from time to time, but, unable to compete with the larger Leagues, and despoiled of their best players, they have been forced to withdraw. Under a new regime there are at present quite a number of these minor organizations, and some of them are in a most flourishing condition.

In 1882 the National League, American Association, and Northwestern League entered into what was called the "Triparti Agreement," which the following year was developed into the "National Agreement." The parties to this document, which is become the *lex suprema* in base-ball affairs, are now, primarily, the National League and the American Association. It regulates the term of players' contracts and the period for negotiations; it provides a fine of five hundred dollars upon the club violating, and disqualifies the player for the ensuing season; it prescribes the formula necessary to make a "legal" contract; the clubs of each Association are to respect the reservations, expulsions, blacklistments, and suspensions of the clubs of the other; it declares that no club shall pay any salary in excess of two thousand dollars; finally, it provides for a Board of Arbitration, consisting of three duly accredited representatives from each Association, to convene annually, and, "in addition to all matters that may be specially referred to them," to have "sole, exclusive, and final jurisdiction of all disputes and complaints arising under, and all interpretations of, this Agreement." It shall also decide all disputes between the Associations or between club members of one Association and club members of the other.

To this main agreement are tacked "Articles of Qualified Admission," by which the minor base-ball associations, for a consideration and upon certain conditions, are conceded certain privileges and protection. These articles are an agreement between the League and American Association, party of the first part, and the minor leagues as party of the second part.

The most important feature of the National Agreement unquestionably is the provision according to the club members the privilege of reserving a stated number of players. No other club of any Association under the Agreement dares engage any player so reserved. To this rule, more than any other thing, does base-ball as a business owe its present substantial standing. By preserving intact the strength of a team from year to year; it places the business of base-ball on a permanent basis and thus offers security to the investment of capital. The greatest evil with which the business has of recent years had to contend is the unscrupulous methods of some of its

"managers." Knowing no such thing as professional honor, these men are ever ready to benefit
themselves, regardless of the cost to an associate
club. The reserve rule itself is a usurpation of the
players' rights, but it is, perhaps, made necessary by
the peculiar nature of the base-ball business, and
the player is indirectly compensated by the improved
standing of the game. I quote in this connection
Mr. A. G. Mills, ex-President of the League, and
the originator of the National Agreement: "It
has been popular in days gone by to ascribe the de-
cay and disrepute into which the game had fallen to
degeneracy on the part of the players, and to blame
them primarily for revolving and other misconduct.
Nothing could be more unjust. I have been identi-
fied with the game more than twenty-five years—for
several seasons as a player—and I know that, with
rare exceptions, those faults were directly traceable
to those who controlled the clubs. Professional players have never sought the club manager ; the club
manager has invariably sought—and often tempted
—the player. The reserve rule takes the club manager by the throat and compels him to keep his
hands off his neighbor's enterprise."

It was not to be expected that club managers of
the stamp above referred to would exhibit much
consideration for the rights of players. As long as
a player continued valuable he had little difficulty,
but when, for any reason, his period of usefulness to
a club had passed, he was likely to find, by sad experience, that base-ball laws were not construed for
his protection ; he discovered that in base-ball, as in
other affairs, might often makes right, and it is not

to be wondered at that he turned to combination as a means of protection.

In the fall of 1885 the members of the New York team met and appointed a committee to draft a Constitution and By-laws for an organization of players, and during the season of 1886 the different "Chapters" of the "National Brotherhood of Ball-Players" were instituted by the mother New York Chapter.

The objects of this Brotherhood as set forth by the Constitution are :

"To protect and benefit its members collectively and individually ;

"To promote a high standard of professional conduct ;

"To foster and encourage the interests of ' The National Game.' "

There was no spirit of antagonism to the capitalists of the game, except in so far as the latter might at any time attempt to disregard the rights of any member.

In November, 1887, a committee of the Brotherhood met a committee of the League, and a new form of players' contract was agreed upon. Concessions were made on both sides, and the result is a more equitable form of agreement between the club and players.

The time has not yet come to write of the effect of this new factor in base-ball affairs. It is organized on a conservative plan, and the spirit it has already shown has given nothing to fear to those who have the broad interests of the game at heart. That it has within it the capacity for great good, the writer has no manner of doubt.

And thus the erstwhile schoolboy game and the amateur pastime of later years is being rounded out into a full-grown business. The professional clubs of the country begin to rival in number those of the halcyon amateur days ; and yet the latter class has lost none of its love for the sport. The only thing now lacking to forever establish base-ball as our national sport is a more liberal encouragement of the amateur element. Professional base-ball may have its ups and downs according as its directors may be wise or the contrary, but the foundation upon which it all is built, its hold upon the future, is in the amateur enthusiasm for the game. The professional game must always be confined to the larger towns, but every hamlet may have its amateur team, and let us see to it that their games are encouraged.

CHAPTER I.

THEORY OF THE GAME.—A CHAPTER FOR THE LADIES.

On account of the associations by which a professional game of base-ball was supposed to be surrounded, it was for a long time thought not a proper sport for the patronage of ladies. Gradually, however, this illusion has been dispelled, until now at every principal contest they are found present in large numbers. One game is generally enough to interest the novice ; she had expected to find it so difficult to understand. and she soon discovers that she knows all about it ; she is able to criticise plays and even find fault with the umpire ; she is surprised and flattered by the wonderful grasp of her own understanding, and she begins to like the game. As with everything else that she likes at all, she likes it with all her might, and it is only a question of a few more games till she becomes an enthusiast. It is a fact that the sport has no more ardent admirers than are to be found among its lady attendants throughout the country.

Whoever has not experienced the pleasure of taking a young lady to her first game of ball should seize the first opportunity to do so. Her remarks about plays, her opinions of different players and the umpire, and the questions she will ask concerning the game, are all too funny to be missed. She is a violent partisan and at once takes strong sides, and if her favorite team fails to bat well she characterizes the opposing pitcher as a " horrid creature ;" or when the teams have finished practicing she wants to know, with charming ingenuousness, " which won." But as she gets deeper into the principles of the game her remarks become less frequent and her questions more to the point, until her well-timed attempts to applaud good plays and the anxious look at critical points of the game indicate that she has at last caught the idea.

Unfortunately, some men are not able to intelligibly explain the theory of base-ball, while others are so engrossed with the game that they do not care to be disturbed. For the benefit of those ladies whose escorts either cannot, or will not, answer their questions, I will attempt to set forth as clearly as possible the fundamental principles of the game.

There are always two opposing teams of nine players each, and they play on a field laid out in the shape of a diamond, as seen in the diagram on the following page.

At each corner of the diamond is a base, and these are known respectively as home base, first base, second base, and third base. One of the teams takes " the field," that is, each of its nine players occupies one of the nine fielding positions shown in the diagram, and known as pitcher, catcher, first base, second base, third base, short stop, left field, centre field, and right field ; the other team goes to " the bat " and tries to make " runs." A run is scored in

Diagram of Ball Field, showing position of Players, etc

Centre

Left

2d Baseman

Short Stop

3d Baseman

1st Baseman

Coacher

45½ ft.

PITCHER

4 ft.

90 feet

6 ft.

Batsman

1 ft.

Batsman

6 ft.

50 ft.

4 ft.

4 ft.

50 ft. line

50 ft. line

CATCHER

C

UMPIRE

C

A

A

Catcher's fence

A. A. A.—Ground reserved for Umpire, Batsman, and Catcher.
C.—Players' Bench.

this way : One of the nine batting players takes his position at the home base and endeavors to hit the ball, thrown to him by the opposing pitcher, to some part of the field where it can neither be caught before touching the ground, nor thrown to first base before the batter himself can run there ; if he can hit it far enough to allow him to reach not only first base, but second or third or even home, so much the better, for when he has made the complete circuit of the bases his side is credited with one run. If he cannot make home on his own hit he may be helped around by the good hits of succeeding batsmen, for each one of the nine takes his regular turn at the bat. This batting and running goes on until three of the batting side have been " put out," whereupon the batting side take the field and the other team comes in to take its turn at bat and make as many runs as possible. When three of a batting side have been " put out," that side is said to have had its "inning," and each side is entitled to nine innings.

A player is " put out " in various ways, principal among which are the following : If he strikes three times at the ball and misses it and on the third strike the ball is caught by the catcher ; a ball which passes over the plate between the height of the knee and shoulder and not struck at, is called a strike just as though it had been struck at and missed. The batsman is also " out " if the ball which he hits is caught by some fielder before touching the ground ; or if, having touched the ground, it is thrown to the first-baseman before the batter himself can reach that base. He is out if, at any time after having hit the ball, he is touched with it in the hands of a fielder, when no part of his person is touching a base.

There are lines drawn from the home base through the first and third-base corners and continued indefinitely into the field. These are called "foul lines," and any hit ball falling outside of them counts as nothing at all, unless, of course, it be caught before touching the ground, in which case it puts the striker "out."

Outside of the nine players on each side there is another important personage, known as "The Umpire." He is not placed there as a target for the maledictions of disappointed spectators. He is of flesh and blood, and has feelings just the same as any other human being. He is not chosen because of his dishonesty or ignorance of the rules of the game, neither is he an ex-horse thief nor an escaped felon ; on the contrary, he has been carefully selected by the President of the League from among a great number of applicants on account of his supposed integrity of character and peculiar fitness for the position ; indeed, in private life he may even pass as a gentleman.

His duties are arduous ; he must decide all points of play, though taking place on widely separated portions of the field ; he determines whether a ball has been fairly pitched over the home-base, whether a hit is "fair" or "foul," or whether a player has been put out in accordance with the rules. In brief, he is expected to see all parts of the field at once and enforce all the principal and incidental rules of the game. It would not be strange, therefore, if he made an occasional mistake or failed to decide in a way to suit all.

I have given thus concisely, and with the use of as few technical terms as possible, the first principles of the game. Many things are purposely left for the novice to learn, because any attempt to go into detail would prove confusing. For the instruction of those who wish to master the technical terms generally used, I subjoin some definitions. They are intended for beginners, and though not in all cases covering the entire ground, will yet convey the idea.

DEFINITIONS.

A *batsman*, *batter*, or *striker* is the player who is taking his turn at bat.

A *base-runner* is what the batter becomes instantly after having hit a fair ball, though for convenience of distinction he is often still called a batter until he has reached first base.

A *fielder* is any one of the nine fielding players.

A *coacher* is one of the batting players who takes his position within certain prescribed limits near first or third base to direct base-runners and to urge them along.

A *fair hit* is, generally speaking, a ball hit by a batsman which falls within the foul lines.

A *foul hit* is one which falls without the foul lines.

A *base hit* is a fair hit by a batsman which can neither be caught before touching the ground nor fielded to first base in time to put out the striker. It may be either a two-base hit, a three-base hit, or a home run, according as two or three or four bases have been made on the hit without an intervening error.

An *error* is made when a fielder fails to make a play that he should fairly have been expected to make.

A *fly* is a hit caught before touching the ground.

A *muff* is made when a "fly" or thrown ball, striking fairly in the hands of a fielder, is not caught.

A *grounder* is a hit along the ground.

A *steal* is made when a base-runner gets from one base to another without the assistance of a base hit or an error.

A *wild pitch* is a ball thrown by the pitcher out of the fair reach of the catcher, and on which a base-runner gains a base.

A *passed ball* is a throw by the pitcher which the catcher should stop but fails, and by his failure a base-runner gains a base.

For the purpose of distinction, the nine fielders are subdivided into The Battery, The In-field, and The Out-field. The *Battery* means the Pitcher and Catcher, the *In-field* includes the First, Second, and Third Basemen, and the Short-stop, and the *Out-field* is composed of the Left, Centre, and Right Fielders.

As for the theory of the game, remember that there are opposing sides, each of which has nine turns at the bat, *i. e.*, nine innings, and the object each inning is to score as many runs as possible. A run is scored every time a player gets entirely around the bases, either by his own hit alone or by the help of succeeding batters, or by the errors of the opposing fielders, and the team making the most runs in nine innings is declared the winner. An inning is ended when three of the batting side have been "put out," and a player may be put out in various ways, as before enumerated. The umpire is not trying to be unfair, he is doing the best he can, and instead of abuse he is often deserving of sympathy.

CHAPTER II.

Some one has truthfully said, that ball players, like poets and cooks, are born, not made, though once born, their development, like that of their fellow-artists, may be greatly aided by judicious coaching. Of what this training shall consist becomes then a question of much importance.

The only way to learn base-ball is to play it, and it is a trite saying that the best practice for a ball player is base-ball itself. Still, there are points outside of the game, such as the preliminary training, diet, and exercise, an observance of which will be of great advantage when the regular work is begun. The method and style of play and the points of each position are given in the subsequent chapters, so that I shall here speak only of those points which come up off the field and are not included in the game proper.

But first of all, let me say, that no one will ever become an expert ball player who is not passionately fond of the sport. Base-ball cannot be learned as a trade It begins with the sport of the schoolboy, and though it may end in the professional, I am sure there is not a single one of these who learned the game with the expectation of making it a business.

There have been years in the life of each during which he must have ate and drank and dreamed base-ball. It is not a calculation but an inspiration.

There are many excellent books devoted exclusively to the general subject of training, and a careful reading of one such may be of much service in teaching the beginner the ordinary principles of self-care. It will show him how to keep the system in good working order, what are proper articles of diet, how to reduce weight, or what exercises are best calculated to develop certain muscles ; but for the specific purposes of a ball player such a book is entirely wanting, for the reason that the "condition" in which he should keep himself, and therefore the training needful, differ from those for any other athlete. To perform some particular feat which is to occupy but a comparatively brief space of time, as to run, row, wrestle, or the like, a man will do better to be thoroughly "fit." But if the period of exertion is to extend over some length of time, as is the case with the ball player, working for six months at a stretch, his system will not stand the strain of too much training. Working solely on bone and muscle day after day, his nervous system will give way. he will grow weak, or as it is technically known, "go stale." This over-training is a mistake oftenest made by the young and highly ambitious player, though doubtless many of the instances of " loss of speed " by pitchers and "off streaks " by older players are really attributable to this cause.

The "condition" in which a ball player should keep himself is such that his stomach and liver are in good order, his daily habits regular, his muscles free and firm, and his " wind " strong enough to allow him to run the circuit of the bases without inconvenience. He must not attempt to keep in what is known as "fine" condition. He should observe good hours, and take at least eight hours sleep nightly; and he may eat generously of wholesome food, except at noon, when he should take only a light lunch. There are many players who eat so heartily just before the game that they are sleepy and dull the entire afternoon. The traveling professional player needs to pay particular attention to the kind and quality of his food. The sudden changes of climate, water, and cooking are very trying, and unless he takes great care he will not get through a season without some trouble. Especially should he avoid under or over ripe fruit, for it is likely that many of the prevalent cases of cholera morbus are due to indiscretions in this particular.

If he finds it necessary to take some light stimulant, let it be done *with* the evening meal. Never take any liquor at any other time. I do not favor the indiscriminate use of any drink, but, on the contrary, oppose it as a most harmful practice ; I do believe, however, that a glass of ale, beer, or claret with one's meal is in some cases beneficial. A thin, nervous person, worn out with the excitement and fatigue of the day, will find it a genuine tonic ; it will soothe and quiet his nerves and send him earlier to bed and asleep. The "beefy" individual, with plenty of reserve force, needs no stimulant, and should never touch liquor at any time. If taken at all, it should be solely as a tonic and never as a social beverage.

The force of the above applies with special empha-
sis to the young professional player. Knowing so
well the numberless temptations by which he is surrounded, I caution him particularly against indiscriminate drinking. In no profession in life are
good habits more essential to success than in base-
ball. It is the first thing concerning which the wise
manager inquires, and if the player's record in this
respect is found good it is the most hopeful indication
of his future success. *Keep away from saloons.*

The amount of work necessary to keep a player in
the proper form must be determined in each particular case by the individual himself. If he is inclined
to be thin a very little will be enough, and he should
not begin too early in the spring ; while if prone to
stoutness he may require a great deal, and should
begin earlier. It is scarcely necessary to say that all
exercise should be begun by easy stages. Com-
mencing with walks in the open air and the use of
light pulley weights or clubs or bells, the quan-
tity of exercise may be gradually increased. Never,
however, indulge in *heavy* work or feats of strength.
Such exercise is not good for any one, but especially
is it dangerous for ball players. They do not want
strength, but agility and suppleness ; besides, the
straining of some small muscle or tendon may inca-
pacitate one for the entire season, or even perma-
nently. Right here is the objection to turning loose
a party of ball players in a gymnasium, for spring
practice. The temptation to try feats of strength is
always present, and more than likely some one will
be injured.

The best preliminary practice for a ball player,

outside of actual practice at the game, is to be had in a hand-ball court. The game itself is interesting, and one will work up a perspiration without noticing the exertion ; it loosens the muscles, quickens the eye, hardens the hands, and teaches the body to act quickly with the mind ; it affords every movement of the ball field except batting, there is little danger from accident, and the amount of exercise can be easily regulated. Two weeks in a hand-ball court will put a team in better condition to begin a season than any Southern trip, and in the end be less expensive to the club.

But whatever preliminary work is found advisable or necessary to adopt, the player should be particular in the following : Having determined the amount of exercise best suited to his temperament, he should observe regular habits, keep the stomach, liver, and skin healthy, attend carefully to the quality of food taken, and if he takes any stimulant at all let it be with the evening meal.

CHAPTER III.

THE PITCHER.

Of all the players on a base-ball nine, the pitcher is the one to whom attaches the greatest importance. He is the attacking force of the nine, the positive pole of the battery, the central figure, around which the others are grouped. From the formation of the first written code of rules in 1845 down to the present time, this pre-eminence has been maintained, and though the amendments of succeeding years have caused it to vary from time to time, its relative importance is more marked to-day than at any preceding period. In a normal development of the game the improvement in batting would unquestionably have outstripped the pitching, and finally overcome this superiority; but the removal of certain restrictions upon the pitcher's motions, the legalization of the underhand throw instead of the old straight-arm pitch, the introduction of "curve" pitching, and, finally, the unrestricted overhand delivery, have kept the pitching always in the lead. At several different times, notably in the rules of 1887, an effort has been made to secure a more even adjustment, but recent changes have undone the work, and the season of 1888 will see the inequality greater, if anything, than ever.

The qualities of mind and body necessary to constitute a good modern pitcher are rarely combined in a single individual. First-class pitchers are almost as rare as prima donnas, and out of the many thousand professional and amateur ball players of the country not more than a dozen in all are capable of doing the position entire justice.

Speaking first of the physical requirements, I will not discuss the question of size. There are good pitchers of all sizes, from Madden and Kilroy to Whitney and McCormick, though naturally a man of average proportions would have some advantages.

The first thing necessary before one can become a star pitcher is the ability to throw a ball with speed. The rules, which at present govern the pitching, place a premium on brute strength, and unless one has a fair share of this he will never become a leading pitcher. There are a few so-called good professional players whose sole conception of the position is to drive the ball through with all possible speed, while others whose skill and strategy have been proven by long service, are forced out of the position because they have not sufficient speed for the modern game.

Next, one must be possessed of more than an ordinary amount of endurance. It is by no means a simple task to pitch an entire game through and still be as effective in the ninth inning as in the first ; and when, as sometimes happens, the contest is prolonged by an extra number of innings, the test is severe. This being true of a single game, how much more tiresome it becomes when continued regularly for an entire season, during the chilly days of the spring and fall, and under a broiling July sun, can be ap-

preciated only by one who has gone through it. And
what with all day and all night rides from city to
city, broken rest and hasty meals, bad cooking and
changes of water and climate, the man is extremely
fortunate who finds himself in condition to play every
day when wanted.   Only a good constitution, a vig-
orous digestion, the most careful habits, and lots of
grit, will ever do it.

Besides force and stamina, there are certain mental
characteristics necessary.   A pitcher must be possessed of courage and of self-control.   He must face
the strongest batter with the same confidence that he
would feel against the weakest, for it is only so that
he can do himself entire justice ; and he must be able
to pitch in the most critical situations with the same
coolness as at any other stage.   He must control his
own feelings so as not to be disconcerted by anything
that may happen, whether through his own fault, that
of a fellow-player, or through no fault at all. He should
remember that all are working for a common end,
and that the chances of victory will be only injured
if he allows his attention to be diverted by unavoidable accidents.   And then, too, it is more manly to
play one's own game as best one can, no matter what
occurs, than to continually display an ugly temper
at the little mishaps sure to occur in every game.

The next point is to acquire a correct position in
the "box," and an easy, yet deceptive, style of delivery.   The position is, to a great extent, prescribed
by the rules, and so much of it as is not can be
learned by observing the different pitchers. The position which seems most natural should be chosen. The
ball should be held in exactly the same way, no mat-

ter what kind of curve is to be pitched. Being obliged
by rule to keep the ball before the body, in sight of
the umpire, any difference in the manner of holding it
will be quickly noticed by a clever batter, and if for a
particular curve it is always held in a certain way,
he will be forewarned of the kind of ball to expect.

JOHN CLARKSON.

Some batters pay no attention to these little indica-
tions; but the majority are looking for them all the
time, and once they detect any peculiarities, they will
be able to face the pitcher with much greater confidence. The correct manner of holding the ball for
every kind of delivery is between the thumb and the

4

first and middle fingers, as shown in the accompanying cut of Clarkson.

It is true there are some curves which may be better acquired by holding the ball differently in the hand, but this fact is outweighed by the other considerations of which I have just spoken. Pitcher Shaw might still be a "wizard" had he not neglected this precaution ; by noticing his manner of holding the ball the batter always knew just what was coming ; and there are other pitchers yet in the field who would find their effectiveness greatly increased by a closer observance of this point.

As for the style of delivery, it should be remembered that the easiest movement is the best. A long, free sweep of the arm, aided by a swing of the body, will give more speed, be more deceiving to the batter, and allow of more work than any possible snap or jerky motion. Facing the striker before pitching, the arm should be swung well back and the body around so as almost to face second base in the act of delivery ; this has an intimidating effect on weak-nerved batters ; besides, not knowing from what point the ball will start, it seems somehow to get mixed up with the pitcher's arm and body so that it is not possible to get a fair view of it. It will be understood what motion is meant if there is an opportunity to observe Whitney, Clarkson or Keefe at work.

Next comes the knowledge of how to throw the different curves. I have yet to see an article written on this subject which is of the least value in instructing a complete novice. In the chapter on " Curve Pitching " will be found the theory of the curve, but as for describing intelligibly the snap of the wrist

and arm by which the various twists are imparted
to the ball, I am convinced it cannot be done, and
will waste no effort in the attempt. To curve a ball
is not a difficult feat, and a few practical lessons,
which any schoolboy can give, will teach the
movement. But, while not attempting myself to tell
how this is done, to one already possessed of the
knowledge, I may offer some valuable suggestions.

Not only must the ball always be held in the
same way before pitching, but in the act of delivery
the swing of the arm must be identical or so nearly
so that the eye of the batter can detect no difference.
All this means that the pitcher must not give the
striker the slightest inkling of the kind of ball to expect, so that he will have the shortest possible time
in which to prepare to hit. I advise against the use of
too many different curves. The accomplished twirler
can pitch any kind of curve, but there are some which
he seldom employs. It is impossible to be accurate
when too many deliveries are attempted, and accuracy is of far greater importance than eccentric curves.
Almost all professional pitchers now use the over-
hand delivery and pitch only a fast, straight ball and
a curve. The fast ball, on account of its being
thrown overhand and the twist thereby given,
"jumps" in the air, that is, it rises slightly, while
the curve, pitched with the same motion, goes outward and downward. The curve will necessarily be
slower than the straight ball, and this will give all
the variation in speed needed to unsettle the batter's
"eye" and confuse him in "timing" the ball.
Some pitchers are able, keeping the same motions, to
vary the speed even of the curve and straight balls,

but, as before said, this is apt to be at the expense of
accuracy, and should not be attempted by the young
player. Occasionally, say once an inning, a pitcher
may make a round arm or underhand motion simply to
mislead the batsman, and if the game is safely won
he may use an underhand delivery if he finds it
rests his arm, but these are exceptional instances.

I have already spoken of the importance of accuracy, but it cannot be too strongly emphasized.
The more marked the control of the ball the greater
will be the success, for no matter how many wonderful curves he may be able to get, unless he has
perfect command he will never be a winning
pitcher ; seasoned batsmen will only laugh at his
curves and go to first on balls. To acquire thorough
control requires long and patient practice. A pitcher
should always pitch over something laid down to represent a plate, and if possible get a batter to stand
and hit against him. Let him practice with some
method, pitching nothing but a straight ball, and trying to put it directly over the plate every time. He
should not be annoyed if the batter hits him, as he
is only practicing. When a pitcher is able to cut the
centre of the plate eight times out of ten he may
begin with his curve and work it in the same way.
Finally, when he can also control the curve, he should
try to alternate it with a straight ball. He will
find that he cannot do this at first and retain command of each, but he should keep at it, an hour or
more *regularly* every day, till he can

Up to this point he has been learning only the
mechanical part of pitching, and if he has learned
it well he is now ready to try his skill and met-

tle on the field of actual contest. And here comes in
an element not before mentioned, which is called
strategy, or "head-work." It means the attempt to
deceive the batter, to outwit him so that he cannot
hit safely. This may be accomplished in many ways,
though the particular way best suited to each case can
only be determined at the time by the pitcher himself.
It depends, therefore, upon his own cleverness and
wits, and it is not possible for any one else to supply
these for him. An intelligent catcher may help him
greatly, but there will still remain many points which
he himself must decide. I may be able, however, to
furnish some hints which will indicate the process of
reasoning by which the pitcher may arrive at certain
conclusions; I can point out some things he should
notice, and describe what these generally mean.

SIGNALING.

But first as to the question of "signs." Every
battery, by which is meant a pitcher and catcher,
must have a perfectly understood private code of signals, so that they may make known their intentions
and wishes to one another without at the same time
apprising the opposing players. The first and, of
course, most important of these is the signal by which
the catcher is to know what kind of ball to expect.

There is no necessity of more than one "sign" for
this, because all that any experienced catcher asks is
to know when to expect a fast, straight ball; not
having received the signal for this, he will understand
that a curve is to be pitched, and the difference in
curve or speed will not bother him after a few moments' practice. Until within a few years this sign

was always given by the pitcher, but now it is almost the universal practice for the catcher to give it to the pitcher, and if the latter doesn't want to pitch the ball asked for he changes the sign by a shake of the head. I think the old method was the better, because it is certainly the business of the pitcher not only to do the pitching, but to use his own judgment in deceiving the batsman. He should not act as a mere automaton to throw the ball ; moreover, the catcher has enough of his own to attend to without assuming any of the duties of the pitcher. Of course, if the pitcher is young and inexperienced, while the catcher is seasoned and better acquainted with the weak points of batters, the latter will be the better one to signal. It may be thought that the right of the pitcher to reverse the sign by a shake of the head practically gives him the same control as though he himself gave the signs, but this is not strictly true ; it is impossible for the pitcher not to be more or less influenced by the catcher's sign, and he will often pitch against his own judgment. At least I found this to be true in my own experience, and therefore always preferred myself to do the "signing." If the pitcher gives this sign he must be careful to choose one that will not be discovered by the other side, for there are certain players always watching for such points. Some years ago the Chicago Club gave me the roughest kind of handling in several games, and Kelly told me this winter that they knew every ball I intended to pitch, and he even still remembered the sign and told me what it was. Chicago finished first that year and we were a close second. That point which they gained upon me may have cost Providence the championship, for they beat us badly in the individual series. When I suspected a club of knowing my sign I used a "combination," that is, I gave two signs ; either one of them given separately was not to be understood as a signal at all, but both had to be given together. I found this to work admirably, and it was never discovered by any club, so far as I know. If it be agreed that the catcher is to give this sign, it is still not necessary that the pitcher be entirely influenced by him. The pitcher should rely upon his own discretion, and not hesitate to change the sign whenever his judgment differs from that of the catcher.

There are certain signs which the catcher gives to basemen when there are runners on the bases, and with these, too, the pitcher must be perfectly familiar, so that he may be able to pitch the ball in accordance with what is about to be done. For instance, if the catcher has signaled to the first baseman that he will throw there, he will probably ask the pitcher for an out curve. In order, then, to help him out with the play and give him plenty of room, the pitcher will not only pitch the out curve asked, but he will keep it well out and wide of the plate, so that it can't possibly be hit, and he will pitch it at the height where it may be best handled by the catcher. So, too, if there is a runner on first who is likely to attempt to steal second, he will "pitch for the catcher," and he should shorten his pitching motion so as to give the catcher as much time as possible to throw. When runners "steal" on a catcher it is oftener not so much his fault as the pitcher's. It is almost impossible to make a clean steal of second, even with a very ordinary thrower behind the bat, if the pitcher will not give the runner too much " start."

The pitcher should also receive a signal from the catcher notifying him when to throw to second base to catch a runner leading off too far. This point will, however, be noticed more appropriately under the duties of " The Catcher."

As for the other bases, first and third, the pitcher should look after them himself without any signal from the catcher. I could always stand in the pitcher's position facing the batter and still see out of " the corner of my eye " how much ground the runner on first base was taking. As the baseman is already on the base, there is no necessity of notifying him of an intention to throw, so, watching the opportunity, I would throw across my body without first having changed the position of my feet or body at all. The throw is, of course, not so swift as by first wheeling toward the base and then throwing, but it will catch a runner oftener. " Smiling Mickey " Welch plays the point to perfection, and last season caught many men " napping " in this way. Its advantage is that it is entirely legitimate. Some pitchers, in order to catch a runner at first, make a slight forward movement, visible to the runner but not to the umpire, as if about to pitch. This, of course, starts the runner, and before he can recover, the pitcher has turned and thrown to first. Notwithstanding the strictest prohibition last season of *any* motion even " *calculated* " to deceive the runner, there were umpires weak-kneed enough to allow these balks.

The easiest men to catch are the best base-runners, because they are always anxious to " get away," and they take the most chances. An ambitious runner will keep moving up and down the line trying to get his start. The pitcher should not appear to notice him, pretending to be interested only in the batter, but watching the runner closely all the time. Suddenly, and without the least warning, he should snap the ball to the baseman. If the pitcher will choose a time when the runner is on the move *away* from the base the batter will be off his balance and may be caught before he can recover.

For the third base it may be advisable to have a signal with the baseman to notify him of a throw. It is very seldom possible to catch a runner off third by a throw from the pitcher, though it may sometimes be done. Clarkson and Galvin both accomplish it at times, though they always do it by the aid of a "balk." Clarkson's method is this: With a runner on first and one on third, the man on first will usually try to steal second, and if the ball is thrown there to catch him, the runner on third tries to score. In this situation Clarkson makes a slight forward movement of the body as though about to pitch, and the runner on third, being anxious to get all possible ground, moves forward. With the same motion, and before the runner can recover, Clarkson, by a prior understanding with the third baseman, throws to the base, the baseman meets the ball there, and before the runner has quite realized what has happened, he is "out." I have reason to know the working of this little scheme, because I was caught by it in Chicago last season in a very close game. The "balk" was palpable, and I made a strenuous "kick," but the umpire refused to see it that way.

A pitcher should not be misled by what I have
said into too much throwing to bases. He should
throw only when there is a fair chance of making the
put-out; for all other purposes, as to hold the runner
close to the base, a feint will answer just as well and
does not entail the possibility of an error.

STRATEGY.

A strategic pitcher is one who depends for success
not simply on speed and curves, but who outwits the
batsman by skill, who deceives his eye, and plays
upon his weaknesses. What will be the best method
for a particular case must be decided in each instance by the pitcher himself, and his success will
depend upon his judgment and cleverness. But
while no general rule can be laid down, I may still
be able to offer some useful suggestions.

Assuming that a pitcher has never seen the batters
whom he is about to face, there are certain points
to be noted as each of them takes his place at the
bat. First, his position and manner of holding his
bat should be observed. If he carries it over his shoulder and in an almost perpendicular position, the
chances are that he is naturally a high ball hitter and
is looking for that kind of a pitch, because that is the
position of the bat from which a high ball is most
easily hit. If, on the contrary, he carries his bat in
a more nearly horizontal position, he is ready either
to " chop " over at a high ball, or " cut " under at a
low one, the chances being that he prefers the latter.
Of still more importance is his movement in hitting,
and this the pitcher must try to discover before the
batter has hit the ball at all. An out-curve should be

pitched just out of his reach; being so near where he wants it, it will draw him out and he will make every movement, except the swing of the bat, as in hitting. This movement should be carefully noted. If, in stepping forward to hit, he also steps *away* from the plate toward the third base, it is at once a point in the pitcher's favor. The batsman is timid and afraid of being hit. If, however, he steps confidently forward, almost directly *toward the pitcher*, he is a dangerous man and all the pitcher's skill will be needed to outwit him. Again, if in stepping forward he makes a very long stride, it is another point for the pitcher, because it shows that he is not only anxious to hit but means to hit hard, and such a man is easily deceived. But if he makes a short stride, *keeping easily his balance and standing well upright*, he is more than likely a good hitter, even though he steps away from the plate, and if in addition to stepping short he also steps toward the pitcher, the pitcher should look out for him.

Without going into too much detail I will try to illustrate: If my batter is one who steps away from the plate I will pitch a fast, straight ball in over his shoulder too high and too far in to be hit. The next time he will step still further away, but this time I should put a fast, straight one over the outside corner of the plate. From his position he will probably not be able to reach it at all, or if he does he will hit with no force. I might pitch the next ball in the same place, and then I should consider it time to drive him away from the plate again and I would send the next one in over his shoulder as before. He may hit at one of these high "in" balls, but if he does he will probably not touch it; at any rate, an-

other fast, straight one over the outside corner ought
to dispose of him. It will be observed I have not
thrown a single curve, nor would I to such a batter
except occasionally, say two or three during the
game, and then only to keep him "guessing."

Taking another kind of hitter, suppose that he
steps up in the best form, making a short stride
toward the pitcher, keeping his balance well and his
form erect. As already said, he is a dangerous batter and likely to hit in spite of my best efforts, but I
must do the best I can with him. I therefore observe his manner of holding the bat and note whether
he prefers a high or low ball, and we will say that it
is a low one. I send a couple of low drop curves
just out of his reach. It is just what he wants if he
could only get at them, and the next time he steps
well in toward the plate. This time, however, I send
a fast, straight, high ball over the plate, and if he
hits it at all, it will be in the air. Another fast,
straight, high one might not escape so easily, but I
have two balls called and can't take the chances of
giving him his base. I therefore try it again. If he has
missed that I now have two strikes, and only two
balls, and can afford to throw away a ball or two,
which I do as before by pitching a couple of low
drop curves out of his reach, until his mind is again
fixed upon that point. Then I would probably again
try a fast, high ball on the inside corner of the plate.
These two cases are given merely to illustrate the
line of reasoning, and in practice each would be governed by its own particular circumstances. To avoid
confusing details, I will add only a few observations :
A batter who steps away from the plate, should be

worked on the outside corner ; one who steps in, on
the inside corner ; one who makes a long, vicious
swing at the ball, will be easily deceived by a slow
ball, much more readily than one who "snaps" or
hits with a short, quick stroke ; one who strides long
must necessarily stoop or crouch, and is in bad form
to hit a high ball ; if he swings his bat always in a
horizontal plane, he will not be able to hit a shoulder
or knee ball as well as one who swings in a perpendicular plane, i. e., who "cuts" under at a low ball
and "chops" over-hand at a high ball ; there are
some batters who prefer to hit only at a fast, straight
ball, while others wait for a curve, and in such a case
the pitcher may get a strike or two by pitching what
he will not care to hit at ; some are never ready to hit
at the first ball pitched, so that by sending this in
over the plate a strike may be secured; some are known
as great "waiters," who will only hit when forced,
and these should be forced to hit at once ; others are
anxious and cannot wait, and may be safely "worked"
wide of the plate.   Then occasionally there will be
found a batter who betrays by his manner when he has
made up his mind to hit, and in that case he will let
go at anything within reach ; therefore a ball should
be pitched where he will be least likely to hit it.   If
the pitcher finds a batter facing for a hit to right field,
he should not give him the ball out from him, but
crowd him with it, keeping it on the inside corner,
and it will be almost impossible for him to succeed.

It does not do to work the same batter always in
the same way, or he will discover a pitcher's method.
Sometimes the pitcher must "cross" him and at
times it is even advisable to give him a ball just

where he would like to have it, but where, for that
very reason, he least expects it.

Finally, a pitcher should not be in a hurry to deliver the ball.   As soon as the catcher returns the
ball the pitcher should assume a position as though
about to pitch and stand there ; he should take all
the time the umpire will give him.   This will allow
him to give and receive any necessary signal from the
catcher, it will rest him and thus enable him to hold
his speed, and, finally, it will work upon the nerves
and eyesight of the batter. The batter will grow impa-
tient and anxious, and unless his eyes are very strong
the long strain in a bright light will blear his sight.

FIELDING THE POSITION.

Some pitchers seem to harbor the impression that
nothing else is expected of them but to pitch the ball,
and the effect of this opinion is to diminish their worth
to a very great extent.· A pitcher is just as much a
fielder as any of the other players, and may render his
side efficient service by his ability to properly care for
this part of his work.

I have already spoken of throwing to bases to
catch runners, and it is unnecessary to say anything
further except to again caution against too much of
it.   A pitcher should throw only when there is a
chance of making the put-out.

In fielding ground-hits he must exert considerable
activity on account of the very short time allowed
him.   He should have the courage to face a hard hit,
because on account of the position of the second baseman and short-stop such a hit will generally be safe if
he does not stop it, or at least turn its course.   It is his

place to get all "bunted" hits. It is a mistake to break up the in-field by bringing a third baseman in close to get hits which a live pitcher should be able to field. When a batter who is likely to bunt the ball comes to the bat, the pitcher must be ready at every ball pitched to move in the direction of the third base line, where such hits are always made. There are some pitchers, such as Galvin and Van Haltren, against whom it is not safe to try a bunt, but, as I have said, many others seem to think they are expected only to pitch.

On a hit to the first baseman the pitcher should cover the base, and if the hit is slow or if the baseman fumbles it he may still have time to toss the ball to the pitcher. The pitcher should not wait until he sees the fumble before starting, but the instant the hit is made go for the base ; he will then be there and ready to receive the ball and not be forced to take it on the run. So, too, the occasion may arise when he should cover second or third, where some combination of play has taken the baseman away and left the base uncovered.

In all cases where a runner is caught between bases the pitcher must take part in the play. If the runner is between first and second, the pitcher will back up the first baseman, leaving the short-stop to back the second baseman ; if between second and third, he will back up the third baseman ; and if between third and home, he will back the catcher.

The pitcher must back up the catcher, the first and third basemen, on all throws from the out field. He must not wait until the throw is made before getting in line, but the moment the probability of such a throw arises, he should get there, and then he can see the entire play, and will be sure to get in a line with the throw. In backing up he must not get too close to the fielder he is backing, otherwise what is a wild throw to him will be likewise to the pitcher. He should keep from fifty to seventy-five feet away.

With runners on bases he should be sure that he understands the situation perfectly before pitching, and he must keep it in mind; then, if the ball is hit to him, he need lose no time in deciding upon the proper place to throw it. If his play is to try for a double by way of second base, he should not wait until the baseman gets there and then drive the ball at him with all his might; but he should toss it to the baseman as he runs for the base, timing the speed of the throw so that the baseman and the ball will reach the base together. Thus no time will be lost, and the throw being easy, may be much more quickly and safely handled.

In short, a pitcher should make himself useful wherever he can, and use his wits in fielding as well as in pitching. He should not be disheartened by poor support or unavoidable accidents, but should keep up his courage, and the entire team will be infused with his spirit. There are some pitchers who are not hit hard and yet seldom win because they display such a lazy disposition in the box that they put all the other players to sleep; and, again, there are others not so successful in the matter of base hits, who yet win more games, on account of the aggressive spirit they impart to their fellow-players. Let the pitcher be alive, then, and if he has any "heart" let him show it; let him keep up his spirits, have a reason for every ball pitched, and use his brain as well as his muscle, for it is only in this way that he can ever take a place in the front rank.

CHAPTER IV.

THE CATCHER.

Next after the pitcher, in regular order, comes the catcher. Though the negative pole of "the battery," his support of the pitcher will largely influence the latter's efficiency, and he therefore becomes an important factor in the attacking force. Were it not for the extreme liability to injury, the position of catcher would be the most desirable on the field; he has plenty of work of the prettiest kind to do, is given many opportunities for the employment of judgment and skill, and, what is dearer than all to the heart of every true ball player, he is always in the thickest of the fight. Moreover, his work, unlike that of the pitcher, always shows for itself, and is therefore always appreciated. A pitcher's success depends upon many circumstances, some of which are beyond his own control, so that, no matter how faithfully or intelligently he may work, he must still suffer the annoyance and mortification of defeat. But the catcher has almost complete control of his own play, he is dependent upon no one but himself, and, in spite of everything and everybody, the nature of his work remains the same.

There are some cases in which a steady, intelligent catcher is of more worth to a team than even the pitcher, because such a man will make pitchers out of almost any kind of material. Bennett, the grand-

5   65

est of every-day catchers, has demonstrated this fact in many instances, and I have no doubt that much of the success of the St. Louis pitchers has been due to the steady support and judicious coaching of Bushong.

There are certain qualifications necessary to produce a good catcher, and if a person has any ambition to play the position, he should first examine himself to see whether he is the possessor of these. Here again the size of the candidate seems not to be of vital importance, for there are good catchers, from the little, sawed-off bantam, Hofford, of Jersey City, to the tall, angular Mack, of Washington, and Ganzell, of Detroit. Still, other things being equal, a tall, *active* man should have an advantage because of his longer "reach" for widely pitched balls, and on account of the confidence a big mark to pitch at inspires in the pitcher. Besides, a heavier man is better able to stand against the shocks of reckless runners to the home plate.

More important than size are pluck and stamina, especially if one contemplates becoming a professional catcher. In every well-regulated team nowadays the pitchers and catchers are paired, and the same pair always work together. Perfect team work involves a perfect understanding by each man of all the points of play of the others, and it is believed that a battery will do better team-work where its two ends are always the same. But to be able to work regularly with one pitcher through an entire season, catching every day when he pitches, a catcher will more than once find his powers of endurance strongly taxed ; and if, for real or fancied injuries, he is often obliged to lay off, then, no matter how brilliant his work when he does catch, he will lose much of his value to the team. Certain injuries are inevitable and necessitate a rest, but there are others of minor importance to which some men will not give way. I do not laud this as pure bravado, but because it sets an example and infuses a spirit into a team that is worth many games in a long race. I have the greatest respect and admiration for the Bennetts and the Bushongs of base-ball.

But there are other features necessary before a person can hope to become a first-class catcher. As before said, he has many chances offered for the employment of judgment and skill ; and to make the best use of these he must be possessed of some brains. The ideal catcher not only stops the ball and throws it well, but he is a man of quick wit, he loses no time in deciding upon a play, he is never "rattled" in any emergency, he gives and receives signals, and, in short, plays all the points of his position, and accomplishes much that a player of less ready perception would lose entirely. Two of the best catchers in the country are neither of them remarkable back-stops nor particularly strong and accurate throwers, and yet both, by their great generalship and cleverness, are "winning" catchers. I refer to Kelly, of Boston, and Snyder, of Cleveland. Ewing, of New York, combines with wonderful skill and judgment the ability to stop a ball well and throw it quicker, harder, and truer than any one else, and I therefore consider him the "King" of all catchers—when he catches.

In learning to catch, the first thing, of course, is to

acquire a correct style, that is, an approved position of body, hands, and feet, the best manner of catching a ball, the proper place to stand, how to throw quickly, and the best motion for throwing. After this comes the study of the different points of play. There are as many different styles in detail as there are individual catchers, and yet, through all, there run certain resemblances which may be generalized.

As to the position of the body, all assume a stooping posture, bending forward from the hips, in order better to get a low as well as a high pitch. Some, like Daily, of Indianapolis, crouch almost to the ground, but such a position must be not only more fatiguing, but destroy somewhat the gauging of a high pitch. A catcher should not stand with his feet too widely apart. It is a mistake some players make, but a little reflection will convince a catcher that a man in such an attitude cannot change his position and handle himself as readily as if he stood with the feet nearer together. Besides, on a low pitched ball striking the ground in front of him, it is necessary to get the feet entirely together to assist the hands in stopping it, and this he cannot do if he is too much spread out. These things may appear to be of minor importance, but it is their observance which often makes the difference between a first-class and an ordinary catcher.

A catcher should not stand directly back of the plate, but rather in line with its outside corner; and when he gets (or gives) his sign for the kind of ball to be pitched, he should not, by any movement out or in, indicate to the batter what is coming; there are some batters who glance down at the plate to see, from the corner of the eye, where the catcher is standing. He will have ample time to move after the pitcher has begun his delivery and when the batter's attention is wholly occupied with that. If an out-curve is coming, he should be ready to move out, or if an in-curve, or fast, straight ball, he should be ready to step in. He should not anchor himself and try to do all his catching with his hands, but in every instance, if possible, receive the ball squarely in front of him. Then if it breaks through his hands it will still be stopped by his body.

In catching a high ball the hands should be held in the position shown in the following cut of Bushong, the fingers all pointing upward.

Some players catch with the fingers pointing toward the ball, but such men are continually being hurt. A slight foul-tip diverts the course of the ball just enough to carry it against the ends of the fingers, and on account of their position the necessary result is a break or dislocation. But with the hands held as in this cut there is a "give" to the fingers and the chances of injury are much reduced. For a low ball the hands should be held so that the fingers point downward, and for a waist ball, by crouching slightly it may be taken in the same manner as a high ball.

Some catchers throw more quickly than others because, having seen the runner start, they get into position while the ball is coming. Instead of standing square with the plate, they advance the left foot a half step, and then, managing to get the ball a little on the right side, they have only to step the left foot forward the other half step and let the ball go. To throw without stepping at all is not advisable, be-

cause, on account of the long distance, there would not
be sufficient speed ; to take more than one step occupies too much time, more than is gained by the
extra speed obtained ; so that the best plan and the
one used by the most successful catchers is the one
just described.   It is not however the speed of the

A. J. BUSHONG.

throw alone that catches a base-runner, but the losing
of no time in getting the ball on the way. Some very
ordinary throwers are hard men to steal on, while
others, who give much greater speed to the ball, are
not so dangerous.

A ball may be thrown under-hand, round-arm, or

over-hand. Experience has proven to me that a ball
may be thrown a short distance, as from home to
second, most accurately by a swing of the arm, half
way between a round-arm and over-hand delivery.
My natural style was over-hand, but I have culti-
vated the other until it now comes without difficulty.
I was influenced to make the change by noting the
styles of other players, particularly of Ewing and
O'Rourke. I found that they both got great speed
and accuracy, and I also noticed that they seldom
complained of "lame arm." By being a more continuous swing, it is a more natural motion, less trying on the muscles, and gives greater accuracy on
account of the twist such a swing imparts to the ball,
much on the same principle as does the twist to a
bullet from a rifled gun. I therefore recommend
it for trial at least. When practicing with the
pitcher the catcher should be just as careful about his
style as he would be in a game, for it is while practicing that his habits are being formed. In returning
the ball to the pitcher each time, he should learn to
catch it and bring the arm back, with one continuous
motion of the hands, without making any stops or
angles.

A word about high foul flies, since many of the
catcher's put-outs are from these hits. A ball thrown
directly up into the air by the hand will descend in a
direct line, and may be easily "judged," but a
pitched ball hit directly up is given a tremendous
twist by its contact with the bat, and, in descending,
this twist carries the ball *forward* sometimes as much
as ten, or even twenty feet. Consequently we see
catchers misjudging these hits time after time because

they either do not know this, or fail to take it into consideration.   It is also necessary to know the direction and force of the wind, and this should be noted from time to time during the game by a glance at the flags, or in some equally sure way.

There is one more point in fielding the catcher's position upon which a few words will not be amiss, that is, as to touching a runner coming home. There is a difference of opinion as to the best place for the catcher to stand when waiting for the throw to cut off such a runner. The general practice is to stand a couple of feet from the plate toward third base and in front of the line.   But this necessitates the catcher's turning half-way round after catching the ball before he can touch the runner, and many an artful dodger scores his run by making a slide in which he takes, at least, the full three feet allowed him out of the line.   Many a run is scored when the catcher seemed to have had the ball in waiting.

I believe the best place to stand is a couple of feet toward third and just *back* of the line.   The pitcher saves the time of turning around and has the additional advantage of having the play in front of him, where he can better see every movement of the runner.   When the game is depending upon that one put-out the best place of all to stand is a few feet toward third and directly *on* the line.   From there the catcher can reach the runner whether he runs in front of or behind him, and if he slides he will come against the catcher and may therefore not be able to reach the plate, or, at least, the catcher may delay him long enough to make the put-out.   It is an extremely dangerous play for the catcher, however, and one that he will feel justi-

fied in attempting only when the game depends upon
the put-out. Brown saved the New Yorks a game in
New Orleans last winter by this play, though Pow-
ell, the base-runner, came against him with such
force as to throw him head-over-heels ten feet away.
The object in standing a few feet toward third is to
avoid close plays, for then if the put-out is made at
all there can be no possible chance for the umpire to
decide otherwise.

SIGNALING.

Under the heading of "The Pitcher" I have spoken
of the necessity of a private code of signals between
pitcher and catcher, and I also said it was the general practice now for the catcher to signify the kind
of ball to be pitched, though it is my own opinion
that the pitcher should do this, unless there are
special reasons why it should be otherwise. In giving this sign the catcher, standing with his hands
resting on his knees, makes some movement with the
right hand, or a finger of that hand, or with the right
foot, to indicate an "out" ball, and some similar
movement with his left hand or foot for an "in" ball.
Of course, this may generally be plainly seen by every
one on the field except the batter, whose back is
turned, and this fact has been taken advantage of by
some teams. The coacher, standing at first or third,
makes some remark with no apparent reference to the
batter, but really previously agreed upon, to notify
him what kind of ball is going to be pitched. This
known, the batter has nothing to do but pick out his
ball and lay on to it with all his weight. Some of
the New York players had great sport the past win-

ter in this way at the expense of the California pitchers. It is therefore advisable that some sign be used that is not easily detected.

There are other signals which a catcher must give to basemen to apprise them of his intention to throw. When there are runners on any of the bases, he should not give the sign to the pitcher to pitch until he has glanced quietly around and seen whether any of the runners are leading too far off the bases, and if so, by a prearranged signal notify the baseman that he will throw. This signal should be known also to the pitcher and by every other fielder who may be interested in the play. The pitcher will now send the catcher the ball wide of the plate and at a height where the catcher can handle it easily. The moment he moves to pitch the baseman starts for his base and the proper fielders get in line to back up the throw, if by accident it should be wild. It is very necessary that the pitcher keep the ball out of the batter's reach, otherwise it may be hit to a part of the field left unguarded by the fielders who have gone to back up the throw ; and the fielders must understand the signal or they will not be able to get in line to back up. The complete success of all these plays lies, therefore, in every one knowing and doing his part, and in all working together. A mistake by one, as if the pitcher allows the ball to be hit and it goes safely to a field that would have otherwise been guarded, demoralizes the entire team, and several such mistakes destroy the confidence of the men in team work. In some cases the basemen themselves signal to the catcher for a throw, but in order that every one interested may see the signal and be prepared for the play, it is manifestly better that the catcher alone should give it.

A tricky runner on second will sometimes lead well off for the express purpose of having the catcher throw down, whereupon, instead of returning to second he goes on to third. Whenever a catcher has reason to suspect a runner of this intention he should make a feint to throw to second, and if the runner starts for third the catcher then has him between the bases. The feint must be well made and no time lost afterward in getting the ball either to second or third, according to circumstances. The importance of a play such as this rests not only in the single put-out made, but in the respect for the catcher with which it inspires subsequent runners. They will be exceedingly careful what liberties they attempt to take. A very quick-witted runner, seeing himself caught in this way between the bases, will, of course, try by every means to extricate himself. He may, in turn, make a feint as if to return to second, and when the catcher throws there he will still go on to third; or, he may feint to go to third and manage to return to second. To catch such a man it is necessary to make a second feint to throw to the base nearest him, and this will almost invariably force him to go in the opposite direction. Besides, with each feint the catcher has stepped quickly forward and by the time he has finished the second feint he is almost down to the pitcher's position. The runner is then completely at the catcher's mercy and only an error of some kind will allow him to escape. There are not more than a half dozen catchers in the profession who know how to make this play properly, but there are some, as I have learned by sad experience.

When there are runners on first and third with second unoccupied, and the runner on first tries to steal second, there are several possible plays. The catcher may throw to second to catch the runner going down ; or he may feint to throw there and throw to third to catch that runner leading off ; or he may actually throw toward second, but short of the base, so that the baseman will have a less distance to return the ball home, in case the runner on third starts in. Which one of these plays is to be made the catcher must decide beforehand and notify the basemen by signal, and he will be governed in his decision by the circumstances of the case. If the situation of the game is such that it will make little difference whether the runner on third scores or not, the catcher will, of course, throw to second to make that put-out. But if one run is vital there are other things to be considered. If the runner at third is very slow or one not likely to attempt to run home, he may still throw to second to catch the man from first. But if the runner at third is one who will attempt to score, the catcher must either throw short to second or else feint and throw to third. Whatever he is going to do must be understood thoroughly by all the fielders interested, and to this end he will give the proper signal. As the second baseman and short-stop may also take an important part in this play, it will be spoken of later.

In conclusion let me say, that in order to accomplish anything by these private signals the catcher must have them in such thorough working order that no mistake can possibly occur. This may come only after long and patient practice ; some fielders find it almost impossible to work with signs, but they must be kept at it every day until the code becomes perfectly familiar to them.

CHAPTER V.

THE FIRST BASEMAN.

From the fact that the first baseman has more "chances" to his credit than any other player, it might seem to the casual observer that his is the most difficult position to play; but as a matter of fact most of his chances are of a very simple nature, involving merely the catching of a thrown ball, and an examination of the official averages will show him leading in the percentages year after year. The possibilities of the position, however, have been developing. For many years, and, indeed, until he retired from the diamond, "Old Reliable" Joe Start was the king of first basemen; but, unquestionably, the play of such basemen as Connor, Commisky, and Morrill is a steady improvement, along with the rest of the game. Especially has there been an advance in the direction of fielding ground hits, and it is now not an unusual sight to see a first baseman getting a hit in short right field, and assisting in the put-out at first or second base.

The position demands a tall man. Such a one, by his longer reach, will not only save many wide throws, but, because he is a good mark to throw at, will inspire confidence in the throwers. He must be able to catch a thrown ball, whether high, low, or on either side. As to the surest way of catching, opinions differ; but as to the best way, everything con-

sidered, I hold the same conditions to be true here as
in the case of the catcher; that is, for a high thrown
ball the fingers should point not toward the ball, but
upward, and for a low thrown ball, just the reverse.
If the throw is off to either side, the baseman must
shift his position so as to be able to reach it, and if
it is so far wide that he must leave the base, he
should not hesitate to do so; he should not imagine
that he is tied to the bag. Start was the first
man I ever saw who knew how to leave the base
for a wide throw. He never took the chance of a
long reach for the ball, unless, of course, the game
depended on that one put-out and there was no
time to leave the base and return. He believed, and
with reason, that it was better to first make sure of
the ball and then touch the base, than, by trying to
do both at once, see the ball sailing over into the
side seats.

It is a difficult play when the throw is to the baseman's left, in toward the runner, because of the danger of a collision with the latter. To the average
spectator who may never have had much experience
on the field, these collisions between players may
seem trifling affairs, but they are not so regarded by
the players themselves. In the history of the sport
many men have been seriously injured in this way,
and a few killed outright. For two weeks once I
was obliged to sleep nights in a sitting posture as
the result of a shock of this kind, and it was months
before I recovered entirely from its effects. To avoid
a collision when the ball is thrown in this way many
good basemen stand *back* of the line with the right
foot touching the base, and allow the runner to pass

in front of them. There was one first baseman who
used simply to reach in his left hand and pick the
ball from in front of the runner with as much ease
and safety as though it were thrown directly to him.
I mean McKinnon, poor Al McKinnon! What a
flood of affectionate recollections his name brings
back. Kind-hearted, full of fun, manly, honest, and
straightforward to the last degree, he was one whose
memory will always be green in the hearts of those
who knew him well.

In picking up low thrown balls which strike the
ground in front of the baseman, some become much
more expert than others. One of the best, I think,
is Phillips, who played last season with Brooklyn,
and is now with the Kansas City Club. When the
bound is what is called a "short bound," that is,
where it strikes but a few inches in front of the
hands, the play is really not a difficult one if the
ground is at all even ; but where it strikes from one
to three feet beyond the hands, it requires considerable skill to get it, especially if the ground cannot be
depended upon for a regular bound. In this latter
case the bound is too long for a "pick-up" and too
short for a long bound catch ; so that the only thing
to do is to calculate as nearly as possible where the
ball *should* bound and then try to get the hands in
front of it. It will be found easier to reach the
hands as far forward as possible and then "give"
with the ball, that is, draw the hands back toward
the body in the direction the ball should take on its
rebound. A player should never turn his face away,
even at the risk of being hit, for by watching the
ball all the time, he may be able to change the posi-

tion of the hands enough to meet some slight mis-calculation as to the direction of the bound.

In fielding ground-hits, the same rule applies to the first baseman as to every other fielder; that he should get every hit he possibly can, with the single qualification that he shall avoid interference with other fielders. But as between a possible interference and a failure to go after a ball that should have been stopped, the interference is much to be preferred. There are some basemen who seem to think there is a line beyond which it is forbidden them to go; they act as though they were tied to the base-post by a twenty-foot lariat. Having fielded a ground-hit, the baseman will usually himself run to the base ; but sometimes the hit is so slow or so far toward second or he fumbles it so long that there is no time left for him to do this. In such case he will toss the ball to the pitcher, who has covered the base. In making this play a baseman should not wait until the pitcher reaches the base before throwing, as it loses too much time, and he should not throw the ball at all, because it makes a difficult catch ; but he should pitch the ball easily in front of the pitcher so that he and the ball will both meet at the base. A little practice will make this play plain and simple, and the advantage of doing it in this way will easily be seen.

There are times when, with runners on the bases, the play will not be to first, but to second, third, or home. With a runner on first, many batters try to hit into right field, because with the second baseman forced to cover second for a throw from the catcher, the space between first and second is left almost un-guarded. But if the first baseman will be on the alert for such a hit, and throw the runner out at second, he not only balks the play but frightens following batters from attempting the same hit. With a runner on third and not more than one man out, all the in-fielders will play closer to the bat, so as to throw the runner out at home on an in-field hit; in such case if the batter should strike out, and the third strike be dropped, the first baseman should not go to his base to receive the throw from the catcher, but meet it on the line as near as possible to the plate. He is then able to touch the runner on his way to first and to throw home if the man on third attempts to score on the throw to first. It may be possible to make a double play by first touching the runner to first and then throwing home; but if the runner to first holds back and there is danger of the man from third scoring, it is obviously best to throw home and cut him off, ignoring entirely the runner to first.

Another point in which many basemen are remiss is in backing up. On all throws from left or left-centre field to second base he should get in line with the throw, and on all throws from the same fields to the plate he should also assist in backing up, unless there is some special necessity for guarding his own base.

There is a prevalent belief that it matters little whether a first baseman can throw well or not, but a moment's consideration will show the fallacy of this. There are some plays in which he needs to be a hard and accurate thrower; with a runner on second and a ball hit to the in-field the runner will sometimes wait until it is thrown to first, and then start for third. In such case only the best kind of a return by the first baseman will head him off. So also in long hits to extreme right field he may have to assist the fielder by a throw to third or home.

It will thus be seen that there are points of play at first base which, in the hands of an ambitious fielder, may be developed into very considerable importance.

CHAPTER VI.

THE SECOND BASEMAN.

Second base is the prettiest position to play of the entire in-field. In the number of chances offered it is next to first base, and in the character of the work to be done and the opportunities for brilliant play and the exercise of judgment, it is unsurpassed. It is true the second baseman has more territory to look after than any other in-fielder, but on account of the long distance he plays from the batter he has more time in which to cover it. The last moment allowed a fielder to get in the way of a ball is worth the first two, because one will be consumed in getting under headway. Then, too, the distance of his throw to first is generally short, and this allows him to fumble a hit and still get the ball there in time. So that while much of his work is of a difficult kind, he is more than compensated by certain other advantages, and, so far as the percentage of chances accepted is concerned, he generally leads every one except the first baseman.

The position should have a man of at least average physical proportions. There are in every game a number of throws to second from all points of the field, and with a small man there many of them would be "wild," on account of his lack of height and reach ; moreover, a larger man offers a better mark to throw at, and the liability to throw wildly

84

is decreased because of the increased confidence on
the part of the throwers. Then, too, a small man is
not able to stand the continual collisions with base-
runners, and as a number of his plays are attempts to
retire runners from first, he grows timid after awhile
and allows many clever sliders to get away from
him.

On the other hand, the position requires a very
active player, and for this reason, too large a man
would not be desirable   On account of the large field
he has to cover, he must possess the ability to run
fast and to start and stop quickly ; he must be able
to stoop and recover himself while still running, and
be able to throw a ball from any position.   Not
all his throws are of the short order ; sometimes
he is expected to cut off a runner at third or return
the ball to the catcher for the same purpose, and in
these cases speed and accuracy are of the utmost importance.

Because of the number and variety of plays that
fall to his lot, he must be a man of some intelligence.   With runners on the bases, the situations
of a game change like the pictures in a kaleido-
scope, so that there is not always time to consider
what is the best play to make ; there are times when
he must decide with a wit so quick that it amounts
almost to instinct, for the loss of a fraction of a second may be the loss of the opportunity, and that one
play mean ultimate defeat.

The exact spot to play, in order best to cover the
position, will be determined by the direction in which
the batter is likely to hit, by his fleetness, and by the
situation of the game.   If there are no runners on the

bases the consideration of the batter will alone determine ; if he is a right-field hitter the second baseman will play more toward the first baseman, the entire in-field moving around correspondingly ; and if he is a left-field hitter he will play toward second and back of the base, in either case playing back of the base line from fifteen to fifty feet, depending upon whether the batter is a very fleet or slow runner. If there are runners on the bases this fact will have to be taken into consideration ; for example, with a runner on second the baseman must play near enough to "hold" the runner on the base and not give him so much ground that he can steal third ; or if there is a runner on first and the baseman is himself going to cover the base in case of a steal, he must be near enough to get there in time to receive the catcher's throw. On the other hand, he must not play too close or he leaves too much open space between himself and the first baseman ; and, though playing far enough away, he should not start for the base until he sees that the batter has not hit. It is not necessary that he be at the base waiting for the throw, but only that he make sure to *meet* it there. Pfeffer, of Chicago, plays this point better than any one, I think, and in all respects in handling a thrown ball, he is unexcelled.

To catch a runner attempting to steal from first, most second basemen prefer to receive the ball a few feet to the side of the base nearest first and in front of the line. The first is all right because it allows the runner to be touched before getting too close to the base and avoids close decisions ; but I question the policy of the baseman being in front of the line in every instance. From this position it is extremely difficult to touch a runner who throws himself entirely out and back of the line, reaching for the base only with his hand. With a runner who is known to slide that way, I believe the baseman should stand back of the line ; it demoralizes the runner when he looks up and finds the baseman in the path where he had expected to slide, and it forces him to go into the base in a way different from what he had intended and from that to which he is accustomed. The veteran Bob Ferguson always stood back of the line, and more than once made shipwreck of my hopes when I might have evaded him if he had given me a chance to slide. The time taken in turning around and reaching for the runner is often just enough to lose the play, whereas, standing back of the line, this time is saved, and, in addition, the baseman has the play and the runner's movements in front of him.

With a runner on third and not more than one out, the batter may try to hit a ground ball to the in-field, sacrificing himself but allowing the runner from third to score. To prevent this the in-fielders will generally play nearer the bat, so as to return the ball to the catcher in time to cut off the runner, and how close they must play will depend, of course, upon the fleetness of the runner. Even then the ball may be hit so slowly or fielded in such a way as to make the play at the plate impossible, in which case the fielder will try to retire the batter at first.

With runners on first and third the one on first will often try to steal second, and if the catcher throws down to catch him, the one on third goes for home.

To meet this play on the part of the runners is by no means easy, but it can nevertheless be done. If the one run will not affect the general result of the game, it may be well to pay no attention to the runner from third and try only to put out the one from first, thus clearing the bases. But if it is necessary to prevent the run scoring, the second baseman must be prepared to return the ball to the catcher in case the runner starts for home. In order to gain as much time as possible, he should take a position to receive the catcher's throw ten feet inside of the base-line; keeping one eye on the ball and the other on the runner at third, if he sees the runner start for home, he must meet the throw as quickly as possible and return the ball to the catcher; if the runner does not start, the baseman should step quickly backward so that by the time the ball reaches him he will be near enough to the base-line to touch the runner from first. The play is a difficult one and requires more than the ordinary amount of skill and practice. There is another and, I think, better way of making this play, which will be spoken of under "The Short-stop," because that player is principally interested.

Before the enactment of the rule confining the coachers to a limited space the coacher at third base sometimes played a sharp trick on the second baseman. When the catcher threw the ball, the coacher started down the base-line toward home, and the second baseman, seeing only imperfectly, mistook him for the runner and returned the ball quickly to the catcher. The result was that the runner from first trotted safely to second, the runner at third remained there, and everybody laughed except the second baseman.

In fielding ground-hits the second baseman, because of his being so far removed from the bat, has a better chance to "judge" a hit. He is able either to advance or recede a step or more to meet the ball on a high bound; and on account of the short throw to first he may take more liberties with such a hit; it is not absolutely necessary that he field every ball cleanly, because he may fumble a hit and still make his play. In general, however, he should meet a hit as quickly as possible, so that if fumbled he may have the greatest amount of time to recover and throw. He should also, if possible, get squarely in front of every hit, thus making his feet, legs, and body assist in stopping the ball in case it eludes his hands. When not possible to get directly in front of the ball he must still try to stop it with both hands or with one, for he may then recover it in time to make the play.

Having secured the ball, he should wait only long enough to steady himself before throwing. He should not hold the ball a moment longer than is necessary. In some cases he has not time to straighten up before throwing, but must snap the ball underhand; and where he gets the hit near enough to the base he should not throw at all, but *pitch* the ball to the baseman; this makes the play much safer. When there is a runner on first and the ball is hit to the second baseman, he tries for a double play, and there are four ways in which it may be made. First, if he gets the ball before the runner from first reaches him he may touch the runner and then throw to first base before

the batter gets there. Second, if the runner from first
stops so that he can't be touched, the baseman drives
him back toward first as far as possible and throws
there in time to put out the batter ; the other runner, being then caught between the bases, is run
down, completing the double. Third, if the hit is
near enough to the base he may touch second and
then throw to first to head off the batter.   And,
fourth, he may first pass the ball to the short-stop,
who has covered second, and the latter throws to first
in time to put out the batter. In nine cases out of
ten the last is the safest play ; it makes sure of the
runner to second and is more likely to catch the batter, because the short-stop is in better shape to throw
to first than the baseman would be if he attempted
to make the play unassisted.

The second baseman should take not only all fly
hits in his own territory, but also all falling back of
the first baseman, and back of the short-stop toward
centre field.   In all these cases he gets a better view
of the ball than either of the other players named,
because, instead of running backward, as they would
be obliged to do, he runs to the side, and the catch is
thus easier for him.   If the hit is one which can be
reached by an out-fielder, and the latter calls that
he will take it, the second baseman will, of course,
give way, because the fielder has the ball in front
of him, in a better position even than the baseman.

With a runner on second he must be on the look-
out for the catcher's signal to the pitcher to throw to
second, and on seeing this he must start at once for
the base to receive the pitcher's throw. He must
also watch for the catcher's sign to the second base-

man notifying him of an intention to throw, and while the ball is passing from the pitcher to the catcher, get to the base to receive the throw.

He should "back up" throws to the first baseman whenever possible, leaving his own base to be covered by the short-stop. He should assist the right and centre fielders in the return of long hits, running well out into the field to receive the out-fielder's throw. When plays arise other than those here mentioned his judgment must tell him what to do, and, without neglecting his own position, he must not hesitate to take any part to advance his team's interests.

CHAPTER VII.

THE THIRD BASEMAN.

In the early days of the game, when the pitching was slower and "fair-foul" hits were allowed, the third base position was the busiest and most difficult to play of the in-field. But the changes in the rules, which did away with "fair-foul" hitting, and those which introduced the present pace in pitching, have taken away much of the third baseman's importance. Most of the in-field hitting now is toward short-stop and second base, and the best of third basemen are not able to average over three or four chances to a game. But, though the amount of his work has been diminished, it still retains its difficult nature. The length of the throw to first, and the short time given him in which to make it, occasion many wild throws, and if he fumbles the ball at all, the opportunity is lost. Fleet runners who hit left-handed, and others who merely "bunt" the ball, can be caught only by the quickest and cleanest work ; so that, everything considered, it is not surprising to find the third baseman generally at the foot of the in-field averages.

A third baseman, like a second baseman, should be a man of at least average size, and Denny, who is by long odds the best in the profession, is a large man. He will have a longer reach for both thrown and batted balls, he will be a better mark to throw

at, and, by reason of his superior weight, he will
have more confidence in the face of reckless base-running. But not every player of proper size who can
stop a ball and throw it accurately to first is capable
of becoming a good third baseman. The New York
team of 1887 demonstrated the odd fact that a man
who seemed entirely unable to play second base,
could yet play third in good style, while another who
was but an average third baseman could take care of
second equal to any one. The explanation probably
lies in the fact that the positions require men of different temperaments. At second base a player of
nervous tendency grows anxious waiting for the ball
to come, and by the time it reaches him is unable to
get it in his hands, while at third base, where the
action is much quicker, such a man is perfectly at
home, because he is not given time to become nervous. The same curious fact is seen when an in-
fielder is changed to an out-field position ; he finds
it impossible, at first, to stop ground-hits, because
they seem never to be going to reach him, and
he is completely "rattled" by the long wait. For
the same reason the most difficult hits which an in-
fielder has to handle are the slow, easy, bounding
balls that under ordinary circumstances a child could
stop.

The proper place for a third baseman to play must
be governed by the nature of the case. For an ordinary right-hand batter, likely to hit in any direction,
and no one on the bases, he should play from fifteen
to twenty feet toward second and several feet back of
the base line. For a very fast runner he should
move nearer the batter, and, if there is danger of a

"bunt," he may even have to play well inside the diamond, though, as before said, all such hits *should* be attended to by the pitcher. For a batter who hits along the foul-line, he will play nearer his base, and for one who invariably hits toward right-field, he will move around toward second base, going, in some instances, even as far as the short-stop's regular position. For left-hand hitters he will generally have to play nearer the bat, because these players always get to first quicker than right-hand batters. They are five or six feet nearer first base, and by the swing of the bat they get a much quicker start. If there is a runner on third and not more than one out, he will have to play near the base before the ball is pitched, the object being to give the runner as little start as possible, so that he cannot score on a sacrifice hit. When the ball is pitched the baseman runs off to his proper position, unless, of course, he has received a signal from the catcher to expect a throw.

The third baseman should go after not only all hits coming within his position proper, but also all slow hits toward short-stop, for the latter is sometimes unable to field such hits in time to make the put-out, on account of the longer distance he plays from the home base. The baseman should, however, avoid useless interference with the short-stop, and he should not put down one hand or otherwise balk that player on a hit plainly within the latter's reach.

Having stopped a batted ball, he should throw it as quickly as possible after having regained his balance, so that if the aim be slightly inaccurate the first baseman may have time to leave the base and return. If there is a runner on first, the baseman's throw

will be to second ; this will, at least, cut off the runner from first, and possibly a double play may be
made, if the ball can be sent to first ahead of the
striker. If there are runners on both first and
second at the time of the hit, he may either
throw to second for the double play as before,
taking the chance of catching two men, or he may
make sure of one man by simply touching the
third base, forcing out the runner from second.
Finally, there may be a runner on third and not more
than one out, in which case, if the runner on third
starts home, he will usually try to cut him off by a
throw to the catcher, though possibly he may still
deem it best to throw to some other base. In any
case, what is the best play he must determine for
himself, and he will expedite his decision by having a
thorough understanding of the situation before the
play arises.

The third baseman should receive a signal from
the catcher when the latter intends throwing to him
to catch a runner "napping." The runner always
takes considerable ground in order to score on a slow
hit to the in-field, or on a short passed ball. By a signal, received before the pitcher delivers the ball, the
baseman knows that the catcher will throw, and during the delivery he gets to the base to receive it. And
here, again, the best base runners are oftenest caught
because they take the most ground. If the batter hits
at the ball the runner takes an extra start, and a quick
throw to the base will very often catch him before he
can get back. It should, therefore, be understood that,
in every case when the batter strikes at the ball and
misses it, the catcher will throw to third, whether or

not he has previously given the signal. In touching a runner the baseman must not run away from him ; he must expect to get spiked occasionally, for, if he is thinking more of his own safety than of making the put-out, he will lose many plays by allowing runners to slide under or around him.

CHAPTER VIII.

THE SHORT-STOP.

Originally, it is said, the short-stop's chief function was as tender to the pitcher, though this soon became an unimportant feature of his work. The possibilities of the position as a factor in field play were early developed ; such fielders as George Wright and Dick Pearce soon showed that it could be made one of the most important of the in-field. But the same legislation which almost crowded the third baseman out of the game, affected materially the short-stop's work, and it is only within the past couple of years that he has regained his former prominent place.

During 1887 there was more hitting to short than to any other in-field position ; though the second baseman averaged more "total chances," on account of a greater number of "put-outs," the "assists" were in favor of the short-stop.

The conception of the position has also undergone some changes, and when, therefore, I say that the position is now played more effectively than ever, it is not to assert that the players of the present are better than those of the past, but simply that these changes have been in the line of improvement, that the short-stop now makes plays never thought of in former years—in short, that the development of the position has kept pace with the rest of the game.

In the early days short-stop was played on the

base line from second to third, or even several feet
inside the diamond ; now it is played from ten to
twenty and sometimes thirty feet back of the line.
The result is a vast increase in the amount of territory covered ; hits are now fielded on either side
which once were easily safe ; short flies to the out-
field, which formerly fell between the in and out-
fielders, are now, many of them, caught ; the short-
stop backs up the second and third bases, helps
"hold" a runner on second, and, on a throw from
pitcher or catcher, the second base is covered by him
almost as often as by the baseman himself. Playing
so much further from the batter, he will make more
errors ; he can seldom fumble a hit and still make
the play ; his throw to first is longer, and must therefore be swifter and more accurate ; but for these dis-
advantages to himself he is repaid many fold by an
increased usefulness to his team. All these features
together make the position very different from what
it was some years ago, and in point of effectiveness
it has undoubtedly been improved.

A short-stop should be a player of more than ordinary suppleness and activity. He has a large amount
of ground to cover ; he has to field sharply hit balls
on either side, and must therefore be able to start
and stop quickly ; he is often obliged to stoop, recover himself, and throw while running, and so has
no time to get his feet tangled. Moreover, his presence is often required at widely separated portions of
the field, with very brief intervals allowed him for
making the changes. He may have to field a hit to
first from near second base, and at once, in continu-
ation of the same play, back up third on the return

of the ball from first base. Or, from a close in-field position one moment, he may be called the next to far left-field to assist in the return of a long hit. So that he needs to be awake all the time and able to transfer himself without delay to that part of the field in which his services are required. On account of the length of his throw to first base, and because he is often expected to assist in the return of a long hit to the out-field, he should be a good, hard thrower. He should also be able to throw from any posture, because there are occasions when he has no time to straighten up and pull himself together before throwing.

In chances for skillful plays and the employment of judgment, short-stop is second to no other position on the in-field. He is tied to no base, but is at liberty to go anywhere he may be most needed, and he is thus able to make himself very useful at times, in plays altogether out of his position proper. But to make the best use of these advantages he must be possessed of some intelligence and a wit quick enough to see the point and act before the opportunity has passed. Brains are as much a necessity in base-ball as in any other profession. The best ball players are the most intelligent, though, of course, natural intelligence is here meant and not necessarily that which is derived from books.

The proper place for the short-stop to play will be governed always by the particular circumstances, as explained in the preceding chapters with reference to other in-fielders. If there are no runners on the bases, regard for the batter alone will determine, but if there are runners, this fact, and the situation of the game, must be taken into consideration. A glance at the diagram of the field given in Chapter I will show the usual position of all the fielders, but from these points they may greatly vary. If the batter generally hits along the left foul-line, the short-stop will play nearer the third baseman, and if, on the other hand, the batter hits toward right-field, the short-stop will move toward second, even going so far as to be directly back of the pitcher, the entire in-field, of course, moving around correspondingly.

If the batter is a heavy runner, the short-stop may play a deep field, because he will still have sufficient time to get the ball to first; and so, also, if there is a runner on first, he may play well back, because his throw then, on a hit, is only to second base. If he is covering second base either to catch a runner from first or to hold a runner on second who has already reached there, he must play near enough to the base to be able to receive the throw. Or, if the attempt is to be made to cut off at the plate a runner trying to score on a sacrifice hit, he will play on the base-line or a few feet inside the diamond.

All in-fielders, as well as out-fielders, should be willingly guided as to the position to play by a signal from the pitcher. The latter, knowing what kind of ball he is going to give the batsman to hit, is best able to judge beforehand of the direction of the hit.

The short-stop should cover second base in all cases where there is a runner on first and the batter is one likely to hit to right-field. This allows the second baseman to guard the territory between second and first, which he would not otherwise be able to do, and if the ball is hit to him, he throws to the short-stop at second, forcing out the runner from first.

He should also guard second when there is a runner on that base and the baseman is obliged to play well off for a hit toward right-field. Of course, he does not play *on* the base, but near enough to be able to reach it if the pitcher or catcher wishes to throw there.

Another instance in which he may take the base is when there are runners on first and third and the runner on first starts for second. One way of making this play was described in speaking of "The Second Baseman," but it is believed that it may be much better done with the assistance of the short-stop. With runners on first and third, the catcher signals whether he will make a long or short throw toward second. When the runner on first starts down, the second baseman runs inside the diamond to a point in line with the base, and the short-stop goes to the base. If the throw is long, the short-stop receives the ball and touches the runner, or returns it quickly to the plate if the runner on third starts in. If the throw is short, the second baseman receives the ball and returns it to the catcher ; or, if the runner on third does not start home, the baseman may still have time to turn and toss the ball to the short-stop to catch the runner from first. In deciding to give the signal for a short or long throw, the catcher is guided by the circumstances of the case and the situation of the game. If one run is going to materially affect the result of the game, the throw will be short, so that the ball may be surely returned to the catcher before the runner from third scores. If the run is not vital, the throw may still be short if the runner at third is speedy ; but if he is slow and not likely to chance the run home, the throw will be all the way to the short-stop to put out the runner from first. The success of the play lies in the fact that the runner on third can never tell, until too late, whether the throw is to be short or long. The play was first made in this way by Gerhardt and myself in 1886, and during the past two seasons it has been tried in the New York team many times with the best results. Each player must, however, understand his part and all work together. In a recent game against Philadelphia, on the Polo Grounds, Crane, who had never taken part in the play before, gave Fogarty a ball within reach and he hit it through the short-stop position, left unguarded by my having gone to cover second base.

On all hits to left and left centre-fields, the short-stop should take second, allowing the baseman to back up the throw, and on all hits to right and right centre the baseman will take the base and the short-stop attend to the backing up.

In fielding ground hits the short-stop should observe the general principles for such plays. He should, if possible, get directly and squarely in front of every hit, making his feet, legs, and body assist in stopping the ball, in case it gets through his hands.

If the ball comes on a " short bound," he should not push the hands forward to meet it, but, having reached forward, " give " with the ball by drawing back the hands in the direction the ball should bound. In this way if the ball does not strike the hands fairly, its force will at least be deadened so that it will fall to the ground within reach of the player ; whereas, if he pushes his hands forward and

the ball does not strike fairly, it will be driven too
far away.

He should meet every hit as quickly as possible,
so that if fumbled he may still have time to recover
the ball and make the play. In running in to meet
the ball, he must not forget the importance of steadi-
ness, and to this end should get himself in proper

form just before the ball reaches him. What is meant
by "good form" may be seen by the above cut.
The feet, legs, hands, arms, and body are all made to
assist in presenting an impassable front to the ball.

If base-ball diamonds were perfectly true the
bound of the ball might be calculated with mathe-
matical precision, but unfortunately they are not,
and these precautions become necessary.

There should be an understanding between the

short-stop and third baseman that the latter is to take
all slow hits toward short, and as many hard hits as
he can fairly and safely field.   The effect of the baseman's covering ground in this way is to allow the
short-stop to play a deeper field and farther toward
second base.   Some players do not like the idea of
another fielder taking hits which seem more properly
to belong to themselves, but this is the correct way
for a short-stop and third baseman to work, and between two men, playing only for the team's success,
there will never be any dispute.

It is always best, when possible, to use both hands
to stop or catch a ball ; but sometimes a hit is so far
to either side, or so high, that it can only be reached
with one hand.   Therefore, a short-stop should *practice* one-hand play so that he may be able to use it
when the emergency requires.   He should never attempt it at any other time.

Having secured a batted ball, he should throw it
at once, waiting only long enough to regain his balance and make sure of his aim.   The practice of
holding the ball for a moment and looking at the runner, whether done to demonstrate the fielder's perfect *sang froid*, or to make a swift and pretty throw
for the benefit of the grand stand, is altogether
wrong. Generally, the throw will be to first, though
sometimes there will be an opportunity to put out
another runner, in which case it will be to some other
base.   In throwing to second or third, if he is near
the base, he should pass the ball to the baseman by
an easy, underhand toss.   It is a difficult play to
catch a *thrown* ball when the thrower is quite near ;
besides, in making double plays by way of second base,

any time lost in tossing the ball will be more than regained by the quicker handling, and there is the additional inducement of safety.

In making double plays to second it is almost always better to pass the ball to the baseman and allow him to throw to first, than for the short-stop to attempt to make the play alone. In 1882, a couple of weeks before the season closed, the Providence Club reached Chicago with the pennant all but won ; one game from Chicago would have made it sure. In about the sixth inning of the last game, with the score four to two in our favor, the first two Chicago batters reached their bases. Kelly then hit to George Wright at short, who passed the ball to Farrell, retiring the runner from first, but Jack threw a little high to Start and missed the double. With runners on first and third, the next man, Anson, hit hard to Wright, so that he had plenty of time again for a double. But, this time, instead of passing the ball to Farrell, as before, George attempted to make the play alone. He touched second, but, by the time he was ready to throw Kelly came against him, and the result was a wild throw, and, to complete the disaster, the ball rolled through a small opening under a gate and both runners scored. We were beaten finally six to five, and lost the championship. It should be added that the game would have been won again in the eighth inning but for the unpardonable stupidity of one of the Providence base-runners.

By far the most difficult catch on a ball field is that of a ball hit high to the in-field, because of the great " twist " to the ball. The slightest failure to get the ball fairly in the hands will result in a miss, and yet this is always greeted by derisive howls from certain among the spectators. There are various styles of catching these hits, but the position of the hands shown in the accompanying cut is believed to be the best.

The hands should be reached well up to meet the ball and then brought down easily in the line of

its course. If the hands and arms are held stiff, the ball will rebound from them as though it had struck a stone. The use of a glove on one hand may be found helpful in counteracting the effect of the twist. The short-stop is expected to try for all such hits falling in his own position, and also all falling back of the third baseman and in short left-field.

With runners on bases, a double play may sometimes be made by allowing such a hit to first strike
the ground. In order that the ball may not bound
beyond reach, it should be caught or " picked up "
on the short bound, and to do this safely requires a
great deal of skill. It is a pretty play, and often of
invaluable service, and it should therefore be prac-
ticed carefully until it can be made with approximate
safety. The short-stop must not betray beforehand
his intention, but pretend that he is going to catch
the ball on the fly.

With all signals given by the catcher to the different in-fielders the short-stop must be perfectly familiar, in order that he may be prepared to do his part.
If there is to be a throw to second or third he should
know it, so that he can be ready to back up in case
the throw is wide or breaks through the baseman's
hands. So, too, he must know when to expect a
throw if he himself be covering second.

In all cases where a runner is caught between
bases, the short-stop must take part. If the play is
between first and second or between second and third,
he and the second baseman alternate in backing one
another up on one side of the runner, while the other
baseman and the pitcher do the same on the other
side. If it is between third and home, he and the
third baseman attend to one side, while the catcher
and pitcher look after the other. In every case the
base runner should be run down as quickly as possible, and always toward the base farthest from the
home plate, so that if an error is made the runner
will gain no advantage.

In backing up other fielders a short-stop may be

of great service, and he should do this in every possible case, no matter where the play may be. But
the positions which he is specially bound to back up
are the second and third bases, not only on all throws
from the catcher, but from any other fielder, where it
is possible for him to get in line with the throw. He
must not get too close to the baseman but keep a
sufficient distance back of him to make sure of getting in front of the ball.

CHAPTER IX.

THE LEFT-FIELDER.

The simplest of the three out-field positions is the left-field, and one evidence of this is seen by the fact that a left-fielder almost invariably leads in the averages.

If fielding were the only consideration, the man who was the surest catch, who could run the fastest and throw the longest, would be the best man for the left-field position ; but other points enter into the question. A team, to win, must have hitters as well as fielders, and it is therefore usual to fill up the out-field with good batters, even at the expense of a slight weakness in fielding.

Considered simply as a fielder, the occupant of the left-field should have a good "eye" to "judge" a ball hit in the air. The moment the hit is made he must be able to tell its direction and locate the place where it is going to fall. The best fielders acquire a remarkable skill in this respect and are able to decide these things at a glance. The fielder who is obliged to keep his eye on the ball all the time it is in the air will not cover nearly so much ground as the one who is able to put down his head and run until near the ball. Particularly is this true of a fly hit over the fielder's head. The player who attempts to run backwards or sideways for the ball, or who turns his back to the ball but keeps his head twisted around so as to see it, will not begin to get the hits that a man will who is able to locate the hit exactly and then turn and run until he has reached the spot where the ball is going to fall. If the eyesight is good any fielder can learn to do this, all it requires being sufficient practice and plenty of confidence.

Another qualification for a fielder is the ability to start quickly and run fast. The player who excels in these respects will, of course, get more hits than one who starts and runs slowly.

Next, he must be a sure catch on a batted ball, no matter in what shape he may be obliged to take it, whether running toward or with the ball, and whether it be high, low, or on either side. Many fielders are sure of a ball if they can get it in a particular position or at a certain height, but this is not enough, for it is not always possible to do this. A player who feels himself weak on any point should practice and practice upon that particular thing until he has mastered it. If he can catch hits on his right better than on his left side, let him practice catching only on the left; if he is weak on hits over his head, he should have some one bat to him thus, until he has overcome the weakness. Any failing of this nature may be corrected by practice.

A fly ball should never be caught holding the hands and arms rigid. The fielder should reach up to meet the ball and then bring the hands down easily with it. There are some balls hit to the outfield, as well as to the in-field, which the fielders cannot possibly reach with both hands but may be able to get with one. In a game played to-day (May 7th), between New York and Indianapolis, Hines, of the latter Club, made a marvelous one-hand catch of a hit that would otherwise have been good for three bases ; and the effect of that one play off the first New York batter was so bracing to the rest of the Indianapolis team that it probably accounted for the strong and winning game they afterwards played. So that, while discountenancing one-hand plays when two hands may be used, I still think every fielder should practice one-hand catches, to be prepared for such a play when it becomes necessary.

In fielding balls hit along the ground, the fielder should not wait until the ball comes to him, but run in to meet it as quickly as possible. Then, if fumbled, he may still have time to get it back to the in-field before base runners can take an extra base.

The instant an out-fielder gets a ball in his hands he should throw it to some point in the in-field. The habit of holding a ball is extremely dangerous. If the bases are clear and a single base-hit is made the ball should be sent at once to second base. If there is a runner on first, it should be thrown to third base, because if sent to second a bold runner will some-times keep right on to third. If there is a runner on second when the hit is made and the left-fielder secures the ball quickly, he should throw it to third, because most runners will over-run that base in order to draw the throw to the home plate, and a quick throw to the base will catch them before they can return.

The left-fielder is expected to back up the second and third bases on a throw from first base or right-field. He should also back up third on a throw from the catcher, and to this end must be on the look-out for the catcher's signal. He must also back up the cen-

tre-fielder when that player runs in to meet a hit,
for, though he may not be able to get in front of the
ball, he will still be able to recover it quicker than
the centre-fielder in case it gets by the latter. He
should also get near the centre-fielder when the latter is trying for a high fly, so that if the ball is missed
he may assist in sending it quickly to the in-field.

As soon as a fielder has decided that he can get to
a hit and has made up his mind to take it, he should
call out loudly and distinctly, "I'll take it." That
gives every one else warning to keep out of the way,
and avoids the chance of collisions. On the other
hand, if he is running for a hit and hears some other
fielder call out, he should reply, quickly and clearly,
"Go ahead." That gives the other fielder confidence,
and he need not hesitate or take his eye from the
ball to learn the location of other fielders. If this
very simple rule is observed there will never be any
collisions, nor will any hits that should be caught be
allowed to drop between fielders.

On all long hits out of the fielder's reach he should
go after the ball with all possible speed and return
it to the in-fielder, who has gone out to help him
back with the ball. If he misses a fly he should get
after the ball at once and send it to the proper point
on the in-field, and not walk after it simply because
he has missed it.

Andy Leonard, of the old Bostons, was, in his day,
one of the best of left-fielders. He was particularly
strong on balls hit over his head, which he always
took over his shoulder while running with the direction of the hit. He was also a remarkably hard
and accurate thrower.

CHAPTER X.

Much of what has been said with reference to the left fielder is applicable also to the occupant of the centre field. As a fielder only, it is necessary that he should possess the same powers of "judging" a hit quickly, of starting the instant the hit is made, of running fast until he has reached it, and of catching the ball in any position ; but as a fielder and *batter* as well, his fielding qualities are often overlooked, to a certain extent, in favor of his power as a batter.

Many fielders prefer to catch a ball while they are running and so regulate their speed as to be still on the move when they meet the ball. Some of them do this because they can catch a ball better in that way, and others because they think it looks prettier and pleases the grand stand ; they are continually making what appear to be difficult catches, and they occasionally fall down and roll over to add to the effect. But while this may deceive the average spectator, it never escapes the other players, and they soon grow extremely weary of such gymnastics. And after awhile the spectators, too, discover his tricks, and then the player will not get credit even for the really good work he may do. Another thing to be said against this grand-stand style of play is that these players sometimes miscalculate the direction or force of a hit

113

just enough to lose it, whereas if they had run hard at first the ball would have been easily caught. The safest plan is to get under the hit as quickly as possible and then there will be time to correct any slight misjudgment.

In fielding balls hit along the ground, the out-fielder should run in quickly to meet the ball and return it instantly to the proper point on the in-field. I have seen games lost by out-fielders stupidly holding a ball or returning it lazily to the in-field. There is absolutely nothing to be gained but everything to be lost by such plays.

In throwing to any point on the in-field, if the throw is at all a long one, the fielder should line the ball in *on the bound*. An out-fielder should never attempt a long throw on the fly, to first or third or home. A throw on the first bound will reach there just as quickly, more accurately, and with less chance of getting by the fielder to whom it is thrown.

The centre fielder must back up second base on all throws from the catcher, and also on throws from any other position, whenever possible. On throws from the direction of first base he will be assisted by the left fielder and from the direction of third base by the right fielder. When a runner is stealing second base and the catcher's throw is wild, the centre fielder must meet the ball quickly so as to prevent the runner from going on to third. In a case of this kind a crafty runner will often make a feint to run to third in order to force the fielder to throw the ball in the hope that he may throw it wild. If there is a probability that the runner actually intends to go to third, there is nothing left the fielder but to throw and take the chance. But if the fielder has good reason to suspect the honesty of the runner's intentions, a quick throw to second, instead of to third, will often catch him before he can return.

The centre fielder should also back up the left and right fielders on all hits along the ground which either of them runs in to meet. It gives one fielder more confidence to go in quickly after a ball if he knows there is another fielder behind him to stop it in case it passes himself.

Even on an in-field hit to the second baseman or short-stop the out-fielder should move in at once, so as to be able to recover the ball quickly if it gets through the in-field.

When a runner is caught between first and second or second and third bases, the centre fielder should get in line with the play, back of second base. For, while only four players take an active part in such a play others should back up to provide for the possibility of a wild throw.

The necessity of "calling" for a fly hit applies with particular force to the centre fielder. As soon as he has seen that he can get to a hit and has decided to take it, he calls out loudly so that every one must hear, "I'll take it," and all the other fielders near him respond, "Go ahead." This will avoid all danger of collisions to which he is specially exposed by having a fielder on either side.

On all high flys to another out-fielder he should go near the fielder who is attempting to make the catch, so that if the ball is missed and bounds his way, he can recover it quickly and prevent runners from gaining extra bases.

CHAPTER XI.

THE RIGHT FIELDER.

The right field, when properly played, is the most difficult of the out-field positions. A ball hit in that direction by a right-handed hitter always describes a curve and is therefore very hard to judge. A good right fielder should also throw out many men at first base during a season, and this means that he must possess all the qualifications of an in-fielder. A few years ago it was not an unusual thing to see a batsman thrown out at first on a hit into right field. One of the best fielders for this was George Shaffer, who for several seasons played with the Cleveland Club. Another good man was "Jake" Evans, of the Troy Club, and when with the Providence Club, Dorgan seldom let a game go by without catching one or more men in this way.

Of late this is not done so often, for the reason that the right fielder plays a much deeper field now than he did a few years ago. Then, when the "curve" was still a novelty, there were very few hard hits made to right field by right-handed batters. Still, even now, there are many batters for whom there is no reason to play a deep right field, and such a batter should often be thrown out at first. Yet the only player whom I have seen make the play this season was Brown, of Boston, who threw out Titcomb twice in one game on the Polo Ground.

All that has been said about the other out-fielders as to judging a hit, starting, running, and catching, may be said of the right fielder. Equally with them he must locate a hit instantly, start quickly, run speedily, and be able to catch the ball in whatever form he may reach it. In judging a hit the fielder always takes into consideration the force and direction of the wind—with the effect of which he has become familiar in the preliminary practice—and the curve which the ball is likely to take if hit by a right-hand batter.

In fielding ground-hits he meets the ball quickly, and, where possible to catch the batter at first, he throws there on the fly. The reason for throwing so in this instance is, that if he is near enough to catch the man at all, he is near enough to throw accurately on the fly. But to third base or home he should always throw on the bound.

He should back up first base on all throws from the catcher. He also should assist the centre fielder in backing up second base, and to this end run back of the centre fielder when the latter goes in to meet the ball ; so that if it passes one, the other will still be there to stop it. He should also back up the centre fielder on all ground-hits to the latter, and on all fly hits to him he should go near so as to quickly recover the ball if it be missed.

He should "call" for the ball the moment he has decided to take it, and as between an out-fielder and an in-fielder the former will take any hit he can reach. He is running in for the ball and has it before him all the time, while the in-fielder, running out, is apt to get twisted up and in bad shape to make the catch.

Out-fielders, like in-fielders, must change position to correspond with the direction the batsman is likely to hit. For instance, there are some men who are never known to hit to right field, and for such the entire out-field moves toward the left field, the right fielder going almost to centre, the centre fielder to left centre, and the left fielder close to the foul-line. When the fielder knows the batsman, he will change without direction ; but in any case he should respond quickly to any signal from the pitcher, because the latter may be going to force the batter to hit in a particular direction. The best fielders make the greatest difference in the positions they play for different batsmen.

The right fielder must be on the look-out for the catcher's signal to throw to first or second base, because, in order that he may get in line with the throw, it is necessary that he shall start when the pitcher begins to deliver. He cannot wait until the catcher throws or he will be too late to get in line.

CHAPTER XII.

THE BATTER.

The most unsatisfactory feature in base-ball to the player himself, is batting. In theory it is so simple, yet in practice so difficult, that one is forever finding fault with himself and thinking, when too late, of what he might have done if only he had not done as he did.

Of course, the element of chance or " luck," as it is called, enters largely into the question. The hardest hit will sometimes go directly into the waiting hands of a fielder, while a little " punk " hit from the handle or extreme end of the bat may drop lazily into some unguarded spot. But, in the course of a season, these chances should about equalize one another, and, though fate may seem to be against a man for a half dozen or more games, he will be found finally to have benefited as much by " scratch " hits as he has lost in good, hard drives.

The theory of batting is simplicity itself. All that is necessary is to wait until the ball comes over the plate and then hit it on a line back into the field. From the grand stand, nothing could be easier. To sit back of the catcher and see the balls come sailing over the plate, one will wonder why they are not hit out of creation, and when some player, who has allowed a couple of balls to pass directly over the plate without making the least attempt to hit at them,

finally lets go at one that he could scarcely reach
with a wagon tongue, much less with a 36-inch
bat, the spectator is likely to question the fellow's
sanity. It is amusing to sit in a base-ball crowd and
hear the remarks. There are more good batters and
umpires and all-round ball players in the grand stand
within one's hearing, than are to be found in both
the contesting teams.

It would be more amusing still if some of these
prodigies could be lifted out of their seats and taken
down into the field, and, with a bat in hand, made to
face some first-class pitcher until they had hit the
ball just once. They would be surprised to see how
differently it looks. At a distance of only fifty feet
from a man who can throw a ball like a streak of
lightning, or with the same apparent motion, send it
so slowly that one will think it is never going to
reach him, who can curve it in or out, up or down,
the question of hitting the ball at all becomes one of
some doubt, to say nothing of " base hits." And
then, add to this the danger of a swift, wild pitch
carrying away an arm or burying itself in the batsman's stomach, and the difficulty is greatly increased.
Just think of it for a moment. A player who can
throw a ball, say one hundred and sixteen and two-
thirds yards, goes into the pitcher's box and from a
distance of only sixteen and two-thirds yards throws
the ball to the batter with all speed. If the throw is
wild and the ball hits the batter it strikes him with a
force that would have been sufficient to carry the ball
one hundred yards further. It would be interesting
to know just how many mule power there is behind
such a blow. There are a few moments after a man

has been hit during which he wishes he had never seen a base-ball, and for the next couple of games, at least, he will think more of escaping a recurrence of the accident than of hitting the ball. Hines, of Indianapolis, has already been hit on the head this season by one of the Chicago pitchers, and the result is a long, ragged-looking scar that he will always carry. An inch lower, and the blow might have cost him his life.

The first consideration in learning to bat is to acquire the proper form. By this is not meant the position to be assumed while waiting for the pitch, because each batter may, and generally does have his distinctive style. But when *in the act of hitting* there is a certain form to be observed, and this, in its salient points, is the same with all good batters.

Standing within easy reach of the plate, the batter should hold his bat ready to hit a breast-high ball. It is easier to hit a low ball when expecting a high one than to hit a high ball when a low one was expected, for the reason that it is easier to drop the bat quickly and swing underhand than it is to elevate it and chop overhand. When the ball is pitched he should not move until he has seen where the ball is going. Not until in the act of swinging his bat should he step forward, and then his step should be short, and, generally, directly toward the pitcher. When he hits, the body should be held erect and flung slightly forward, so that when the bat meets the ball the weight is principally on the *forward* foot.

If he steps too soon, his position is taken and he cannot change it to suit any slight miscalculation he may have made in the speed or direction of the ball.

Neither should he make too long a stride, for the same reasons given in the preceding paragraph, and also because it puts him in bad form to hit at a high ball.

He should generally step directly toward the pitcher, unless he has special reasons for doing otherwise. For instance, if a right-hand hitter wishes to hit to left-field, he had better step so as to face slightly in that direction ; and if he wishes to hit to right-field, he will stand farther from the plate and step in with the left foot so as to face somewhat in the direction he intends to hit.

The object in standing erect is to keep well the balance and be in a position to cut under or over at a low or high ball. The body is thrown slightly forward so that the weight and force of the body may be given to the stroke. It is not necessary to hit hard, but *solidly*, and this is done not so much by the swing of the arms as by the push and weight of the shoulder behind it.

The accompanying cut of Ewing is an excellent representation of a batter, in the act of hitting. He not only swings the bat with the arms, but pushes it with the weight of the shoulders. The position is a picture of strength.

In hitting at a high ball the bat should be swung overhand, in an almost perpendicular plane, and so, also, for a low ball, the batter should stand erect and cut underhand. If the bat is swung in a horizontal plane the least miscalculation in the height of the ball will be fatal. If it strikes above or below the centre line of the bat, it will be driven either up into the air or down to the ground. Whereas, if the bat is swung perpendicularly, the same mistake will only cause it to strike a little farther up or down on the bat, but still on the centre line, and if it misses the centre line it will be thrown off toward first or third, instead of up or down.

There are two classes of good batters whose styles

WILLIAM EWING.

of hitting are so different that they may be said to be distinct. The one, comprising such hitters as Connor, Brouthers, Tiernan, Wise, Fogarty, Whitney, Ryan, Denny, and Fred Carroll, use the full length of the bat, and in addition to the push of the shoulders make a decided *swing* at the ball. In the other, in which are Anson, Kelly, Dunlap, and a few others, the motion is more of a *push* than a swing. Anson, who, if not the best batter in the country, is certainly the surest, seldom does anything but push the bat against the ball, only occasionally making what might be called a swing. Many of the latter class grasp the bat up short, and some of them keep the hands a few inches apart. If I were advising a novice which style to learn I should say the latter, because it is the surer, though such batters seldom hit as hard as the others.

Every ball player who pretends to play the game with his brain as well as with his body, should be able to hit in whatever direction he wishes. It may not be always possible to hit in the exact direction desired, and, of course, he cannot " place " the ball in any particular spot, but he can and should be able to hit either to left field or right, as the occasion demands. The advantage of this to the player himself and to his team cannot be overestimated. For example, there is a runner on first who signals to the batter that he will try to steal second on the second ball pitched. When he starts to run the second baseman goes for his base and the entire field between first and second is left open. Now, if the batter gets a ball anywhere within reach and taps it down toward right field, the chances are that it will be safe, and the runner from first will keep right on to third. Oftentimes, too, the batter himself will reach second on the throw from right field to third to catch the runner ahead of him. Here, now, by a little head-work, are runners on third and second, whereas, an attempt to smash the ball, trusting to luck as to where it should go, might have resulted in a double play or at least one man out and no advantage gained. Many a game is won by such scientific work, and the club that can do the most of it, day after day, will come in the winners in the finish.

When a batter is known as one who will attempt a play of this kind, it is usual for the second baseman to play well over into right field, allowing the second to be covered by the short-stop. When the batter discovers such a scheme to catch him he should continue to face toward right field, in order not to betray his intention, but when the ball is pitched, he should turn and hit toward left field. If the short-stop has gone to take the base, the space between second and third is left open just as the other side was.

A great fault with many batters is that they try to hit the ball too hard. This is especially true of the younger players, the "colts," as they are called. A young player with a reputation as a hitter in some minor league, goes into a big club and at once thinks he must hit the ball over the fence. The result is that he doesn't hit it at all, and unless he corrects his fault, he goes on "fanning the atmosphere" until he is handed his release. And yet the same player, if he would steady himself down and once get started hitting might do just as well as he did in his former club.

And this brings up the reflection that there is a great virtue in *confidence*. The player who goes timidly to the bat with his mind made up that he can't hit, anyhow, might just as well keep his seat. But the one who walks up, saying to himself, "Other men hit this ball, and I can, too," will be inspired

by his own confidence, and for that very reason he
will be more likely to hit. So it is that batting
goes so much by streaks. A nine that has not made
a hit for several innings will suddenly start in and
bat out a victory. One player leads off with a good
hit and is followed by another and another, each
benefited by the confidence and enthusiasm the preceding batters have aroused.

It goes without saying that the player's eyesight
must be perfect or he can never hope to be a good
batter. It requires the keenest kind of an eye to
keep track of the ball and tell when it is over the
plate and at the proper height.

So, too, the nerves must be kept in good condition
or the player will be unable to resist the temptation
to hit at wide balls. A nervous batter is easily
"worked," because he is so anxious to hit that he
can't wait for a good ball.

But the most important attribute of all in the com-
position of a good batter is *courage*. In this term I
include the self-control and the resolution by which a
man will force himself to stand before the swiftest
and wildest pitching without flinching, the fearlessness that can contemplate the probability of a blow
from the ball without allowing the judgment to be
affected. Out of ten poor batters nine are so because
they are afraid of being hit. It is often asked, "Why
are pitchers, as a rule, such poor batters?" and to
this the answer in my own mind has always been
that it is because they know so well the danger which
the batter incurs. There is perhaps no such thing
as absolute fearlessness; the batter who has once
been hit hard—and all of them have—will never quite

forget the occurrence, and he will forever after have the respect for the ball that a burned child has for the fire. But some men will not allow this feeling to overcome them.

It is absolutely necessary, then, to first conquer one's self, to fight down fear and forget everything except that the ball must be hit. To some, this seems not a difficult matter, to many it comes only after the most determined effort and schooling of the nerves, while to a few it seems to be an utter impossibility. The instinct of self-preservation is such a controlling power with them that unconsciously they draw away from the ball, and, try as they will, they cannot stand up to the plate. The player who cannot overcome this feeling will never be a good hitter, though when he finds that he is a victim he should not give up without a struggle. Some players have broken themselves of the habit of running away from the plate by stepping back with the rear foot, instead of forward with the forward foot, when in the act of hitting. Thompson, of Detroit, who is a remarkably good hitter, steps backward instead of forward. Others, like Hecker, of Louisville, step neither way, but hit as they stand, simply throwing the body forward Every expedient should be tried before the case is given up as incurable. In my own case I was forced to change from right to left-hand hitting. I had been hit so hard several times that I grew afraid of the ball and contracted the habit of stepping away from the plate. It was a nervous fear over which I had no control, and the habit became so confirmed that I resolved to turn around left-handed. I thought that in learning to hit the new

way I could avoid the mistakes into which I had before fallen. It took time and practice to learn, but
the result, I think, has been an improvement.
While not able to hit so hard left-handed, because
the muscles are not yet so strong, I make more single
hits, reach first base oftener, and score more runs.

CHAPTER XIII.

THE BASE-RUNNER.

Of the four departments of play, batting, base-running, fielding, and battery work, the most interesting is base-running. It is the most skillful, it calls into play the keenest perception and the soundest judgment, it demands agility and speed, and it requires more daring, courage, and enthusiasm than all the others combined.

Its importance as a factor in winning games cannot be estimated. We only know that a team of base-runners wins game after game in which it is out-batted and out-fielded by its opponents. No system of scoring has been or can be devised by which a full record of this kind of work can be kept. The system now in vogue, crediting the number of bases stolen, is all right so far as it goes, but it covers only a small part of the ground. Stealing bases is a part of base-running, but it is a very small part, and to say that the player who steals the most bases is therefore the best base-runner, is an altogether unwarranted statement. A quick starter, speedy runner, and clever slider might easily steal the most bases, and yet in general usefulness fall far behind some other player.

Beginning with the more mechanical features, the first qualification for a base-runner is the ability to start quickly. The distances on a ball field have been laid out with such marvelous nicety that every fraction of a second is valuable. Almost every play is close, and the loss of an instant of time is often the loss of the opportunity.

But to start quickly means more than a quick action of the muscles ; it means also that the brain and body must act together. The base-runner who must wait to be told what to do will always be too late. By the time the coacher has seen the point and called to the runner and the latter has gotten himself into action, the chance has long passed. The player must be able to see the play himself and act upon it instantly, without waiting to be told.

Different runners adopt different methods for getting a long start from a base. Some take as much ground as possible before the pitch and then start the moment they see the first motion to deliver. Others stand near the base, and when they think it about time for the pitcher to pitch make a start. If they happen to guess aright they get a running start, which is, of course, a great advantage. And if they guess wrong, the pitcher is so taken by surprise that it is always possible to return to the base before he can throw. Of the two methods I prefer the latter. Remaining near the base disarms suspicion, and the runner is not tired out, by repeated feints to throw, on the part of the pitcher.

In either case the practice of standing with the feet wide apart is altogether wrong and in violation of every principle of quick starting. Unlike a sprinter, a base-runner must be in shape to start in either direction, and this can be done best and quickest by standing upright with the feet almost together.

A second qualification is speed. While, as before

said, mere speed will not make a base-runner, in the full sense of the term, yet, other things being equal, the faster runner will be the better base-runner. Straight away running is something to which ball players do not devote sufficient attention. While, to a certain extent, it is a natural gift, yet every man can improve himself greatly by practice, and if the spring training of players included more of this work, the result would certainly be an improvement in the base-running. Notwithstanding the importance of starting and running and sliding, there is absolutely no attention given these matters, and, consequently, the majority of players seem to be entirely ignorant of the proper "form." It would be a good investment for some clubs to employ a professional sprinter to teach their men how to stand, in order to start quickly, and how to put one foot in front of the other in the approved form.

An important aid also to successful base-running is the knack of sliding well. A player skillful in this respect will often save himself when he seems caught beyond escape. Every runner should know how to slide if he expects to accomplish anything at all, and every man will slide who has the proper interest in his work. Some players do not do so because they have never learned and are afraid to try, while others seem to care so little for the team's success that they are unwilling to take the chances of injury to themselves. As for the former class, a half hour's practice on sawdust or soft earth will show them how easily it is learned, and as for the latter, they should be made to slide, even if it be found necessary to persuade them through their pockets.

Sliding, as an art, is of recent growth, though it has long been the practice of base-runners to drop to avoid being touched. In view of its present importance it is amusing to read, in an article written on the subject some years ago, an argument against the practice indulged in by a few players of sliding to the base in order to avoid being touched by the ball.

The old style of sliding was with the feet foremost, but there are now various methods employed. Many runners now slide head foremost, throwing themselves flat on the breast and stomach. Some keep to the base-line and slide direct for the base, while others throw the body and legs out of the line and reach for the base with a hand or foot. Among those who always slide feet first and direct for the base, Hanlon is the most successful. He doesn't go down until quite close to the base, and then does not at all slacken his speed. Connor also slides feet foremost, but instead of throwing himself at full length, he maintains a sitting posture, and each of his slides is the signal for a laugh from the crowd. On account of his size and the weight behind his spikes, he is always given the entire base-line without dispute. Williamson is a very successful slider. He runs at full speed until near the base and then throws his body away from the baseman and his feet at the base. The successful runners who slide flat on the stomach are Fogarty, Tiernan, Miller, Andrews, Brown and others. Of those who go in head foremost but throw the body out of the line and away from the baseman, are Ewing, Glasscock, Pfeffer, Dalrymple and some others.

An expert base-runner will confine himself to no

particular style, but, being familiar with all, will use, in each instance, the one best suited. Sometimes one style is best and sometimes another, depending upon where the ball is thrown and the position of the base-man. I consider Kelly the best all-round slider in the League, because he can, and does, use every style with equal freedom.

The American Association has some of the finest runners in Nicoll, Latham, Stovey, Purcell, and many others, but I have, unfortunately, not seen enough of their work to speak accurately of their methods.

Though stealing bases is only a part of base-running, yet even this requires considerable skill, and it is by no means always the fastest runner who succeeds the oftenest. Much depends on the start, and much, too, on the slide. I may be permitted to outline my own method: Having reached first, I signal to the next batter when I am going to steal. Then, standing near the base, well upright and with my feet together, I try to get a running start on the pitcher; that is, when I think he is about to pitch, though he has yet made no motion, I make my start. If he does pitch I get all the ground that I would have had by playing off the base in the first place, and I have, besides, the advantage of being on the move. Every one who knows anything of sprinting will appreciate the advantages of such a start. If the pitcher does not pitch I usually manage to return to the base in safety. Having secured my start, I expect that the batter will hit the ball, if it is a good one, into right-field, in which case I will keep right on to third base; or, if it is a bad ball, the batter

will at east hit at it, in order, if possible, to blind the
catcher and help me out.   In any event I put down
my head and run direct for the base, and *in no case* do
I attempt to watch the ball.   It is a foolish and often
fatal mistake for a runner to keep his head turned
toward the catcher while running in another direction.   If the ball is hit I listen for the coacher's
direction, but if it is not, I keep my eye on the baseman, and by watching his movements, the expres-
sion of his face, and the direction he is looking, I
can tell as certainly just where the throw is going as though I saw the ball.   If he stands in
front of the line I run back of him, and if he is back
of the line I slide in front.   In every case, and
whether I go in head or feet foremost, I throw my
body away from the baseman so as to give him the
least possible surface to touch with the ball.

There is an advantage in sliding head foremost, in
that the runner, by falling forward, gains the length
of his body and the reach of his arm, whereas. in
sliding feet foremost, he loses this.   But if one always
goes in head foremost, the baseman, knowing what
to expect and standing in no fear of injury, will block
the base-line.   It seems necessary to occasionally
throw the spikes in first in order to retain one's right
to the line and command a proper respect from opposing basemen.

In order that the runner may not be continually
cut and bruised by gravel or rough ground he should
protect his hips and knees by pads.   Some have the
padding stitched to the inside of the pants, and for
the knees this is the better plan, though it interferes
somewhat with the washing of the uniform.   But for

the hips I prefer the separate pads, which may be bought at any store for the sale of base-ball goods. The best make is buttoned to a strap which binds tightly the lower portion of the body, and this latter feature is itself of great advantage; not only as a matter of comfort and safety, but also for the sake of decency, every player should wear one of these straps, the same as athletes do in other branches of sport.

But, after all, the important factors in successful base-running are yet to be spoken of, and the foregoing points are merely mechanical aids. There is no other department of play in which intelligence plays so important a part, and no matter how clever the player as a starter, runner, or slider, these faculties will be of little value unless directed by a quick perception and sound judgment. Indeed, they will often serve only as traps to lead him into difficulty.

By its very nature a quick perception is an inborn faculty of the mind, and while it may be developed by constant use, no amount of coaching can create it. There are some players who are no more capable of becoming good base-runners than of living under water, so unfitted are they by nature. The power of grasping a situation and acting upon it at once is something which cannot be taught.

In order, however, to know when a fair opportunity presents itself, the runner must be familiar with the chances of play, and this comes only from experience and close observation. A runner who is thoroughly alive to all the possibilities of the game will see a chance and gain a point where another of less ready perception would find no opening. The former has learned to marshall at a glance all the attendant probabilities and possibilities and to estimate, in the same instant, the chances of success or failure.

It is not, however, always best to accept an opportunity when presented, even where the chances of success are largely in the runner's favor. The stages of the game must be taken into consideration, and what may be a perfectly commendable play in one situation may be altogether reckless and foolhardy in another. Therefore, the most important faculty of all, the pendulum which regulates, and the rudder which guides, is *judgment*. An illustration may make my meaning clear. In the ninth inning, with a runner on first base and the score a tie, it may be a good play for the runner to attempt to steal second, because from there a single hit may send him home. But suppose that, instead of the score being a tie, the side at bat is four or five runs behind, of what possible use will the steal be now, even if successful? One run will do no good, and the only chance of victory is in the following batters also getting around the bases. But the hits or errors by which this must be accomplished will also send the first runner home without a steal, so that in attempting to steal he takes a chance which is of no advantage if successful, and perhaps a fatal mistake if not.

Again, suppose there is a runner on third and none out and the batter hits a short fly to the out-field, on the catch of which it is doubtful whether the runner can score. If the next batter is a good hitter, he will not make the attempt, trusting to the next hit for a better chance. But if the next batter is weak and not likely to offer as good a chance he may decide to try for the run on the small chance already presented. These are only given as examples and they might be multiplied, because the same problem will always present itself in a more or less imperative form every time the runner has a play to make. The question he must always decide is, "Is this the best play, everything considered?" It goes without saying that he must answer this for himself.

In conclusion, I will describe some plays that may arise and venture some observations, running through which the reader may discern the general principles of base-running.

There is an element in base-ball which is neither skill nor chance, and yet it is a most important factor of success. It is the unseen influence that wins in the face of the greatest odds. It is the element, the presence of which in a team is often called "luck," and its absence a "lack of nerve." It is sometimes spoken of as "young blood," because the younger players, as a general rule, are more susceptible to its influence. Its real name is *enthusiasm*, and it is the factor, in the influence of which, is to be found the true explanation of the curious standing of some clubs. Between two teams of equal or unequal strength the more enthusiastic will generally win. The field work may be slow and steady, but at the bat and on the bases there must be dash and vim.

If, for example, it be found that a catcher is a poor thrower, or a pitcher slow in his movements, every fair runner reaching first should immediately attempt to steal second, and even third. This style of play will demoralize an opposing team quicker than anything else, and even if unsuccessful at first, and the first

few runners be caught, it should still be kept up for a
couple of innings, because it will, at least, affect the
nerves of some of the opposing players, and if a
break does come, the victory will be an easy one.
Every batter should be ready to take his place
quickly at the bat, and hit at the first good ball ;
every runner should be on the move ; and with plenty
of coaching, and everybody full of enthusiasm, it is
only necessary to get the run-getting started in
order to have it go right along.   This is the game
that is winning in base-ball to-day, as every ob-
servant spectator knows.

Base-running begins the moment the ball is hit.
There are some players who don't know how to drop
their bats and get away from the plate.   Some stand
until they see whether the hit is safe, and they run to
first with the head twisted around to watch the ball.
The instant the ball is hit, *no matter where it goes*,
the batter should drop the bat and start for the base ;
leaving the ball to take care of itself, he should put
down his head and run, looking neither to the right
nor the left.   Every foot gained may be of vital importance, for in most cases the runner is thrown out
by the distance of only a few feet.

Some runners make a mistake in jumping for the
base with the last step.   It not only loses time but
makes the decision so plain to the umpire that the
runner fails to receive his fair share of benefit from
close plays.

A runner to first on a base hit or fly to the out-
field should always turn first base and lead well
down toward second, so that if the ball is fumbled or handled slowly or missed, he may be able to

reach second. And by hurrying the out-fielder he increases the probability of an error.

A runner should always run at the top of his speed, except in the single case where he feels himself to be clearly within reach of his base and then slackens up in order to draw the throw.

At no other time is there anything to be gained by slow running, and often there is much to be lost. In the game spoken of elsewhere in this book, between Providence and Chicago, which virtually decided the championship for 1882, Hines was on first when Joe Start hit what looked like a home-run over the centre-field fence. The wind caught the ball and held it back so that it struck the top of the netting and fell back into the field. Hines, thinking the hit perfectly safe, was jogging around the bases when the ball was returned to the in-field. Start had run fast and overtaken Hines, and the result was that instead of a run scored, a man on third and no one out, both runners were put out and we lost the game by one run, and the championship by that one game. A player has no right to " think this or that;" his sole duty is to run hard until the play is over.

When a runner is on first and a hit is made he should run fast to second, and if possible force the throw to third. Every such throw offers an opportunity for error, and the more of these the runner can force the more chances there will be in his favor. By getting quickly to second he is in a position to go on to third if the ball is fumbled or slowly handled, or returned to the wrong point on the in-field.

So, too, a runner on second, when a hit is made, should *always* force the throw to the home plate, even if he does not intend to try for the run. In order to do this he must run hard to third and turn the base as though he really meant to go home. Any hesitation or looking around will fail of the object. The throw home gives the player who hit the ball a chance to reach second base.

In a game where there is plenty of hitting runners should obviously take fewer chances than where the hitting is light.

It is usually advisable for a good runner, who has reached first with two men out, to attempt to steal second, because then one hit will likely bring him home; whereas if he stays on first it will require two hits, or two errors in succession, and these are not likely to come, with two men already out.

The only times to steal third are, first, when there is only one out, for then a hit, a sacrifice, or a long fly will score the run. If there is no one out, the chances are that a runner on second will eventually score anyhow, and if there are two out there is little advantage gained by stealing third. It still requires a hit or an error to score the run, and the same would probably score it from second as easily as from third. Second, it may sometimes be advisable for a runner on second base to steal third, even when there are two out, provided there is also a runner on first. Because, if successful, the runner on first also gets to second, and the result is two stolen bases from the one chance, and a hit will now likely score two runs instead of one.

When there is a runner on second or third with no more than one out, and the batter makes what is apparently a long, safe hit, the runner should hold the base until he has seen, beyond a doubt, that the hit is safe. If safe, he will still have ample time to reach home, while if, by any chance, it be caught, he will nevertheless get third or home, as the case may be. A couple of seasons back a New York runner was on third, with no one out, when the batter made what looked like a home-run hit. The runner on third, instead of waiting to make sure, started home ; the ball was caught and, though he managed to return to third, he did not score, as he otherwise might easily have done. The next two batters went out, the score was left a tie, and we finally lost an important game.

Succeeding base-runners should have private signals so that they may communicate their intentions without apprising the opposing players. A runner on first who intends to steal second should inform the batter, so that the batter may hit the ball, or at least strike at it. A runner on second should notify a runner on first of his intention to steal third, so that the other may at the same time steal second. When there are runners on first and third each should understand perfectly what the other purposes doing so they can help one another with the play.

In such a situation the runner on first will generally attempt to steal second, and if the catcher throws down to catch him there are several things which the runner on third may do. First, as soon as he sees the throw to second he may start for home, and if he has previously decided to do this, he should take plenty of ground from third base. Second, he may not start for home on the throw, but if the runner from first gets caught between first and second, it will then be necessary for him to try to score. For this purpose he carefully takes as much ground from third as possible, while the other player is being chased backward and forward. Finally, when the ball is tossed by the second baseman to the first baseman, he makes a dash for home. The idea of waiting until the ball is thrown to the first baseman is because the latter has his back to the plate, and not only cannot see the play so well but must turn around to throw. Third, if the circumstances are such that he thinks best not to try to score on the throw, he should, at least, on seeing the throw to second, make a strong feint to run in order to draw the second baseman in and allow the runner from first to reach second.

There is a pretty play by which one run may be scored when there are runners on first and second. It is, however, a desperate chance and should only be resorted to in an extremity. The runner on first leads off the base so far as to draw the throw from the catcher, and, seeing the throw, the runner on second goes to third. Then, while the first runner is playing between first and second, the runner now on third scores as described in the preceding play, waiting until the ball is passed to the first baseman. If the second baseman is a poor thrower it may be best to make the dash for home when the ball is thrown to him.

A runner on second may receive a signal from the batsman that the latter intends to try a "bunt," in which case the runner will try to steal third. If the bunt is made the runner reaches third, but if the bunt does not succeed, the attempt draws the third baseman in close and leaves the base uncovered for the runner.

Without particularizing further, it will be seen
that a base-runner must not only have some wits but
he must have them always with him. Exactly the
same combinations never come up, new ones are
continually being presented, and in every case he
must decide for himself what is best. In view of all
the circumstances, he makes a quick mental estimate
of the chances and acts accordingly. Sometimes fortune will be against him, but if his judgment is
sound he is sure to be successful in the majority of
attempts.

CHAPTER XIV.

CURVE PITCHING.

Curve pitching is a scientific fact, the practice of which preceded the discovery of its principle. For a long time after its existence was familiar to every ball-player and spectator of the game, there were wise men who proclaimed its impossibility, who declared it to be simply an " optical delusion," and its believers the victims of the pitcher's trickery. It was only after the curve had been practically demonstrated to them, in a way which left no room for doubt, that they consented to find for it a scientific explanation.

The discovery of the curve itself was purely an accident. During the years from 1866 to 1869 the theory was held by many pitchers that the more twist imparted to a pitched ball, the more difficult it would be to hit it straight out. It was thought that even if it were struck fairly, this twist would throw it off at an angle to the swing of the bat. One writer on the game declared strongly against this practice of the pitchers on the ground that, though this twist did do all that was claimed for it, it at the same time caused the ball, when hit, to bound badly, and thus interfered with good fielding. Of course, both of these theories become absurd in the light of the present, but it was doubtless the belief in the former that led to the introduction of the curve. In 1869 Arthur Cummings, pitching for the Star Club, noticed that by giving a certain twist to the ball it was made to describe a rising, outward curve, and his remarkable success with the new delivery soon led to its imitation by other pitchers, and finally to the general introduction of curve pitching.

The philosophy of the curve is, in itself, quite simple A ball is thrown through the air and, at the

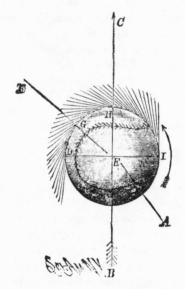

same time, given a rotary motion upon its own axis, so that the resistance of the air, to its forward motion, is greater upon one point than upon another, and the result is a movement of the ball *away* from the retarded side. Suppose the ball in the accompanying cut to be moving in the direction of the arrow, B C, at the rate of 100 feet per second. Suppose, also,

10

that it is rotating about its vertical axis, E, in the
direction of I to H, so that any point on its circumference, I H D, is moving at the same rate of 100 feet
per second. The point I is, therefore, moving forward at the same rate as the ball's centre of gravity,
that is, 100 feet per second, *plus* the rate of its own
revolution, which is 100 feet more, or 200 feet per
second ; but the point D, though moving forward
with the ball at the rate of 100 feet per second, is
moving backward the rate of rotation, which is 100
feet per second, so that the forward motion of the
point D is practically zero. At the point I, therefore,
the resistance is to a point moving 200 feet per
second, while at D it is zero, and the tendency of the
ball being to avoid the greatest resistance, it is de-
flected in the direction of F.

In the *Scientific American* of August 28th, 1886, a
correspondent gave a very explicit demonstration of
the theory of the curve, and, as it has the virtue of
being more scientific than the one given above, I
append it in full.

"Let Fig. 3 represent a ball moving through the
air in the direction of the arrow, B K, and at the same
time revolving about its vertical axis, U, in the direction of the curved arrow, C. Let A A A represent the retarding action of the air acting on different
points of the forward half or face of the ball. The
rotary motion, C, generates a *current of air* about the
periphery of the ball, a current similar to that caused
by the revolving flywheel of a steam engine.

"If, now, at a point on the face of the ball we let
the arrow, R, represent the direction and intensity of
this *rotary current* of air, and if at the same point we

let the arrow, A, represent the direction and intensity
of the retarding action of the air, then we will find
by constructing a parallelogram of forces that the resultant or combined effect of these two currents acts
in the direction indicated by the dotted arrow, T.
In other words, we have a sort of compression, or

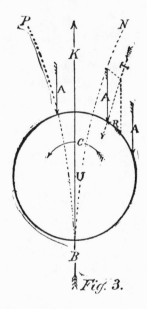

Fig. 3.

force of air, acting on the face of the ball in the direction indicated by the arrow, T. This force, as we
can readily see, tends, when combined with the
original impetus given to the ball, to deflect or cause
the ball to curve in the direction of the dotted line,
B P, instead of maintaining its right line direction,
B K. If the ball rotate about its vert axis in the

opposite direction, the curve, B N, will be the
result.''

To the above demonstrations it is only necessary
to add an explanation of one other feature. The
question has arisen why it is that the ball apparently
goes a part of its course in a straight line and then
turns off abruptly. One might suppose at first
thought that the greater speed at the beginning
would create the greater resistance and consequently
cause the greatest deflection. This, however, is not
true. The difference between the resistance upon
opposite points of the ball in the circumference of
its rotation always *remains the same*, no matter how
great the force of propulsion, and therefore the increased force of the latter at the beginning has no
effect on the curve. But while the force of the twist
itself is not affected by the rate of the forward movement, its effect upon the ball is greatly nullified.
The force of propulsion being so great at first, drives
the ball through the air and prevents it from being
influenced by the unequal resistance. It is only when
the two forces approach one another in strength that
the latter begins to have a perceptible effect. As
soon, however, as it does, and the course of the ball
begins to change, the direction of the dotted arrow,
T, begins to change likewise. It follows the course
of the ball around, and the more it curves the more
this resultant force tends to make it curve, and this
continues until the ball has lost either its twist or its
forward motion.

Having established the fact that a ball will curve
in the direction of the least resistance, it is only necessary to alter the direction of the axis of rotation

in order to change the direction of the curve. Thus, if in the cut first given the ball were rotating in the direction of D H I instead of I H D, the ball would curve, not toward F, but to the right. So, also, if the axis of rotation is horizontal instead of vertical, and the greatest resistance is made to come on top, the ball will curve downward, or "drop." And in the same way, by imparting such a twist that the resistance falls on some intermediate point the ball may be made to take any of the combination curves known as the "outward drop," the "rising out-curve," and so on through the entire category.